THE BURNING WORD
A Christian Encounter with Jewish Midrash

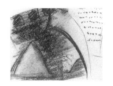

JUDITH M. KUNST

PARACLETE PRESS
Brewster, Massachusetts

2006   First Printing

Copyright © 2006 by Judith M. Kunst
ISBN 1-55725-426-5

Library of Congress Cataloging-in-Publication Data
The burning word : a Christian encounter with Jewish midrash / by Judith M. Kunst.
    p. cm.
ISBN 1-55725-426-5
1. Midrash—History and criticism. 2. Bibile—Meditations. 3. Spiritual life—
Christianity. 4. Kunst, Judith M. (Judith McCune)—Religion. I. Title.
BM514.K865 2006
242'.5—dc22   2005035726

10 9 8 7 6 5 4 3   2   1

Published by Paraclete Press
Brewster, Massachusetts
www.paracletepress.com
Printed in the United States of America.

THE BURNING WORD

16

For my husband and my parents

"Delightful country has fallen to my lot..."
Psalm 16:6, NJPS

Table of Contents

Author's Note   ix

1   Intimacy: Turn & Return   1

2   Reverence: The Word Is Real   15

3   Curiosity: The Word Is Burning   27

4   Community: To Argue Is To Love   39

5   Suffering: The Yeast of Exile   51

6   Attention: To Study Is To Play   63

7   Imagination: Bring the Whole Tithe   75

8   Repetition: The Mirrored Voice   87

9   Truth: Freedom in the Rough   99

10 Creation: A Fire in the Belly   113

11 Revelation: Word Without End   125

Acknowledgments   135

Notes   137

Glossary   149

Author's Note

As an aid to readers who may wish to incorporate elements of Jewish Midrash into their own scripture reading, brief exercises labeled "Toward A Personal Practice" are included in each chapter of this book. These exercises are not drawn from specifically Jewish techniques; rather, they suggest simple actions that aim to help non-Jewish readers usefully translate Jewish ideas into their own faith language and practice.

Many of the exercises contain questions for reflection that can be read, briefly pondered, and put away. Since midrash is at base a conversation with Scripture, however, I invite you to use the questions as a springboard to dialogue, either with a journal or with a trusted friend or group.

1
INTIMACY
Turn & Return

*M*y encounters with Jewish Midrash began when my writing teacher said to me, "You are reading the Hebrew Bible—but are you reading it with Hebrew eyes?" This teacher was not a rabbi; he was not a priest or even a Biblical scholar. He was a writer interested in how language intersects with religion—in other words, how language can shape our experience of, our relationship with, a God we have never seen with our eyes or touched with our hands or talked with face to face.

My teacher did not expect me to answer his question: He knew I was not reading with Hebrew eyes because he knew I was a Christian, as he himself was. But he wanted to suggest to me that the tradition behind my own tradition—Judaism—had something vital to offer me as a writer and reader and seeker after God. This book attempts to describe and share that "something vital" I discovered as I began to explore what it might mean to read the Bible in a different way—a Jewish way.

Perhaps not surprisingly, as I set out to encounter this different tradition, I found myself obliged to honestly and continually encounter my own; I couldn't learn to read in a Jewish way without also clearly defining the way a Christian (at least, this Christian) reads. Two vivid images and two short texts, culled both from my initial experience as a Christian and from my subsequent explorations of Judaism, may help explain what I mean.

The first image is a 1970s style portrait of Jesus, cheaply produced yet lifelike and compelling, which hung in my room throughout my childhood. This Jesus had a friendly face with brown skin, unkempt hippy-like hair, and eyes I could gaze at for hours. Gazing at Jesus never failed to fill me with a mixture of feelings—joy and pain, peace and conflict, life and more life—that I felt nowhere else. Standing in front of that picture was my way of making real the text of an old hymn with which my mother used to sing me to sleep: "Turn your eyes upon Jesus, look full in His wonderful face, / And the things of earth will grow strangely dim / In the light of His glory and grace." As I turned my face toward those kind, brown eyes on the wall, the particulars of my young life fuzzed and faded away. In those moments the things of earth did indeed grow dim, and at the time this seemed not only strange, but wonderful.

My experience of reading the Bible back then, and for many years as an adult, often had a similar kind of "gazing" quality. I would pull the book from the shelf or the pew or the bedside table, open it up either at random or at the thick middle section of Psalms, and flip the pages until I found something that struck me either as familiar or somehow relevant to my own life. Then I would read, sometimes a tiny passage and sometimes a chapter or two. Sometimes I was bored, reading just enough to be able to say I'd done it—fulfilled the mysteriously compelling obligation that evangelical churches had drummed into me since childhood. But sometimes I was far from bored; I was enchanted, pulled into that mysterious space I had come to recognize as uniquely God-filled.

Later, as an adult, I would learn that the ancient Christian name for this kind of Bible reading is *lectio divina*, a form of meditation that allows everything extraneous to leave the mind and heart as the reader gazes on a single verse or word of scripture. But by then I wasn't interested in reading that took me away from what the old hymn called "the things of earth." I wanted a Bible that would not dim or deny but rather sharpen and welcome the particulars of the world I was coming to know, a world of blooming trees and shifting skies, a husband and a child, novels and poems and cancer and war, oceans, mountains, what's for supper, Wall Street, Washington, the lie I told last night. I wanted to embrace these things, and wrestle them into words.

Eventually, I would find in the Jewish tradition a way of reading that vigorously welcomes both language and the world to the arena of scripture study. It's called *midrash*, a Hebrew word meaning "to search out." The Holy Scriptures abound with gaps, abrupt shifts, and odd syntax that puzzles, even confounds, any reader of scripture. Jewish Midrash views these troubling irregularities not as accidents or errors or cultural disparities to be passed over, but rather as deliberate invitations to grapple with God's revealed word—and by extension, to grapple with God himself.

Midrash reads the Hebrew Bible not for what is familiar but for what is unfamiliar, not for what's clear but for what's unclear, and then wrestles with the text, passionately, playfully, and reverently. Midrash views the Bible as one side of a conversation, started by God, containing an implicit invitation, even command, to keep the conversation—argument, story, poem, prayer—going.

Early in my encounters with Midrash, I came across a second image of God to set beside the dreamy-eyed Jesus of my youth. I found it not in a picture on the wall but in the pages of a book: the Talmud, the twenty-volume collection of laws, legends, folktales, and Bible commentary that the Jewish tradition reveres as the vibrant record of its millennia-long conversation with God.

The Talmud says that God himself studies the Bible every day. It says God is sitting in the *bet midrash*, the study house, wearing a round black cap and holding an open Bible, arguing and wrestling his own text right alongside learned rabbis throughout the ages. Here was a God who not only sanctioned my newly daring, honest dialogue with scripture—he wanted to join me.

"Turn it and turn it again," the Talmud says of the scriptures, "for everything is contained therein." This short but potent proverb was written not long after Jerusalem was destroyed in 70 CE, when Jews were scattered abroad and could no longer worship at the Temple, God's dwelling place. A group of surviving rabbis during this upheaval managed to safeguard the Torah, the first five books of the Bible, dictated to Moses and given to Israel on Mount Sinai. They recognized that while the Temple and all its practices were gone, the ancient Book that defined the shape of Jewish life was present, potent, and portable. These rabbis, and later many others who joined them, revered Torah as the place where God had taken refuge, had made a new home. They set about the ingenious and daunting task of reinterpreting its words to help them make sense of a life in exile.

If the Holy One, blessed be he, lives in the scriptures, then no part of its text, no matter how confusing, can be devoid of meaning. Every word, every letter of the text has been put there by divine purpose. Moreover, the tradition assumes, there is no problem or circumstance that cannot be solved by faithful study of Torah. "Turn it and turn it again, for *everything* is contained therein." Anchored in Israel's painful history, the vibrant study practice called midrash puts human imagination to work to illuminate the hidden, holy meanings of scripture, meanings that even today help us make sense of our own confusing, contemporary world.

TOWARD A PERSONAL PRACTICE

Study, imagination, conversation with a hidden God—
each of these can be helped along with pen and paper in
hand. *The ancient records of Jewish Midrash could be most simply described as huge*
communal journals, wherein small sections of the Bible were written out and reflected
upon by many readers. Physically writing or typing out a verse that troubles or
excites you, leaving plenty of blank margins around the words, is a good way to
begin a midrashic conversation with scripture.

If the meaning of scripture is hidden in the text, then language and the tools of language become very important. I sensed this dimly even before I learned about midrash, for after college, without knowing precisely why, I rejected a long-held dream of entering a Christian seminary and enrolled instead in a graduate program to study creative writing. Just a few months before I met the teacher who pointed me toward the Hebrew tradition, I was startled by another teacher's observation.

In class one day this professor handed out excerpts from three different poems: We were to choose one and write our own rhythmically exact imitation. Suddenly she looked at me and said, "Be sure you don't choose the poem from the book of Job." To my quizzical stare she said, "Don't you know you already write in the rhythms of the Bible?" Rhythms. Bible. My writing. How was it that without my awareness the music and pulse of

The Burning Word

ancient Hebrew psalms and stories had reverberated through my reading, into my writing, and out to someone else's ear? I was hungry to know more. Could that mysterious "God-filled space," that powerful swirl of feelings I'd found in a childhood painting of Jesus, be entered more deliberately, explored more concretely, with language?

I started reading my Bible again, not for its comforting, familiar passages, but rather for its language: rhythm, imagery, juxtaposition, all the tools I was experimenting with as a writer. There in my Bible I found writing stranger and more beautiful than anything I myself could hope to compose—and in all that strangeness I found the Creator hiding. *Imagine the branch of an almond tree,* God says to the prophet Jeremiah; *Imagine a broken bowl.* To the prophet Ezekiel he says, *Lie on your side for a hundred days,* and to the prophet Hosea, *Marry your wife three times.* To King David he calls out, *Write me a hundred poems,* and to the exiles Shadrach and Meshach, *Sing me a hymn of fire.* To all Israel God says, *If you seek me, you will ever surely find me,* and then insists: *I will be found by you.*

From the Hebrew Scriptures I moved to a fresh reading of the Greek scriptures—and though I'd been reading them my whole life, I was looking now for strangeness and beauty, reading as a lover of words. "In the beginning was the Word," declares the Gospel writer John, "and the Word was with God, and the Word was God. . . . [T]he Word became flesh and dwelt among us." This image, written roughly around the same time that the ancient rabbis began reinterpreting the Torah, makes an intriguing connection between Judaism and Jesus. Jesus, in John's view, *is* God's language, is in fact God's most ancient and most intimate utterance to us.

The more I learn about midrash, seeking to read the Bible with Jewish eyes, the more the dividing lines start to blur between John's Gospel image, my mother's lullaby hymn, and that early rabbi's Talmudic proverb. These days, to "turn my eyes upon Jesus" can't be separated from turning my eyes upon the words of God's other precious utterance, the Bible—to take *all* its words and turn them, again and again, in my mouth and in my mind and on the blank page before me.

This way of reading does not require technical or scholarly expertise, though such knowledge can richly add to our conversation with the Bible. What midrash does require is close attention, playful imagination, deep reverence, and the courage to continually turn toward the words that trouble us.

What does this mean in actual practice? What does it mean to make midrash?

Summed up simply, making midrash involves four steps: Choose a text. Find in its language a problem or a question. Draw an answer out of your imagination that solves the problem or in some way illuminates new meaning in the text. Then find someone to argue with your interpretation, expand upon it, or propose a different answer altogether.

How to choose a text for midrash? The Jewish practice, like many in the Christian tradition, relies on a long-established calendar of scripture readings: You study the text that is assigned to the particular week in which you find yourself. Some of the oldest Midrash texts, or *Midrashim*, are organized around whole books of the Bible: rabbis interpreting and arguing each successive verse of Genesis or Exodus, etc. Classic rabbinic Midrashim always originated in a verse from Torah— but many people today apply the method more loosely, choosing a text from the Bhagavad-Gita or the Christian Bible, or a poem or passage from a novel.

Though as an adult I married into the Catholic Church, I was raised an evangelical; the latter is a tradition that does not use a calendar of scripture, so my first instinct when making midrash is to choose an already-familiar verse to look at in a new way. Here, for example, is a tiny part of the apostle Paul's prayer in the third chapter of his letter to the Ephesians: *Now to him who is able to do immeasurably more than all we ask or imagine, according to his power that is at work within us, to him be glory.*

A text has been chosen. Where does its language pose a problem or raise a question? This text presents a prayer of praise—"to him be glory"—and also a description of power: This God can act in ways that far exceed our own abilities or perceptions. Why then, I wonder, is the word "immeasurably" tacked onto that description? Doesn't the vivid phrase "more than all we ask or imagine" sufficiently describe God's power?

If I were not seeking to read this text with Jewish eyes, I might dismiss the question as insignificant: Paul just wants to gush about God. But midrash insists that every word of Scripture is there for a purpose; every

Intimacy: Turn & Return

word holds, or hides, meaning. And so I proceed to the third step, calling on the imagination to suggest a reason why that word "immeasurably" is vitally necessary to a deeper understanding of this text.

What does it mean to call on the imagination? It might mean brainstorming, conjuring up a long list of answers, some of which are crazy, some coherent. It can mean making up your own story or new descriptive word. It can also mean opening up one's own mental files of stories, parables, and poems gleaned from the Bible and a host of books and movies and anecdotes, and pulling out one that might shed light on the problem at hand. Whatever the specific approach, imagination always involves some kind of mental leap—often playful, occasionally profound.

Jews of every stripe who sit in a synagogue listening to a sermon may not know it, but often what they're listening to is spoken Midrash. How would a rabbi, then, explain the necessity of the word "immeasurably," in our text? He might start with a story, like this one from the Talmud tractate Seder Eliyahu Zuta, Chapter 2:

> There was a king of flesh and blood who had two servants and loved them both with a perfect love. He gave each of them a measure of wheat and each a bundle of flax. What did the wise servant do? He took the flax and spun a cloth. He took the wheat and made flour. He cleaned the flour and ground, kneaded and baked it, and set it on top of the table. Then he spread the cloth over it and left it until the king would come.

The Burning Word

The foolish servant, however, did nothing at all. After some time, the king returned from a journey and came into his house. He said to his servants: my sons, bring me what I gave you. One servant showed the wheat still in the box with the bundle of flax upon it. Alas for his shame, alas for his disgrace!

When the Holy One, blessed be He, gave the Torah to Israel, he gave it only in the form of wheat—for us to make flour from it, and flax—to spin a garment from it. *11*

This story makes clear the crucial difference between merely safeguarding and actively *using* the gifts of God. It brings to light something hidden in the text we started with: How is God able to do "immeasurably more than all we ask or imagine?" Not by divine might alone, says Paul, but by "his power that is at work within *us*." Only through human effort does the gift of flax become cloth and the gift of flour become bread. To refuse that effort is to refuse the invitation to collaborate with the Creator in the ongoing work of creation.

The king in the Talmud story does not dictate to the servants *how* they should use the gifts they are given. The wise servant could have sold the flax and invested the money for profit, or planted it and reaped more flax for the king. To the wise servant, the possibilities for using the king's gifts are limitless—immeasurable, even.

Now to him who is able to do immeasurably more than all we ask or imagine, according to his power that is at work within us, to him be glory. Hidden in the strange wording of this Biblical prayer of praise to God lies an essential statement about our relationship to that God, and about our own immeasurably creative responsibility and power. I've come full circle with this midrash, answered the question I started with, and gained new insight along the way.

In the Christian tradition the need to make use of God's gifts is one of the Bible's clear teachings, but in rabbinic Judaism, especially as it evolved in the six centuries after the destruction of Jerusalem's Temple in 70 CE, it is the *central* teaching, applied specifically and radically to the act of reading scripture. Bible study has replaced temple worship as the main expression of Jewish religious devotion and communal identity. The word Torah has thus come to be used both as a noun—the content of the scroll found in any synagogue—and as a verb—the entire revelation and the entire activity of Jewish study throughout the generations.

TOWARD A PERSONAL PRACTICE

Find the eighth chapter of Nehemiah in your Bible, and read it out loud. Then consider three questions: What in the language seems strange to you? How might God be hiding in these words? If the verse is imagined to be the first comment in a two-way (or more) conversation, what response from you will keep it going?   .

"Turn it, and turn it again, for everything is contained therein." As a child I thought that turning my eyes upon Jesus called for nothing more than an unblinking gaze and an open heart. Now I see that it requires something more: The wise man took the flax and spun a cloth. He took the wheat and made flour. The ancient rabbis knew what any writer knows, that language must be worked and turned to make something new.

Jewish Midrash asks: What happens when, for hundreds of years, we turn the eyes of our imagination again and again upon a single, holy text? One answer is intimacy— intimacy with the Author of Torah, a God who is at once writer and reader and word, a God who in some sense has given us the Bible for the same reason anyone shares a book with a friend: to start a conversation, to start something new.

Midrash is elusive; no fully accurate and encompassing definition exists, nor have collected translations of the many rabbinic conversations with the text become widely available. There are as many ways to make midrash as there are midrashim. This book, therefore, is not a formal introduction. It is an attempt to capture something of the essential flavor of how Jews read the Bible. Here are a few strands of Biblical flax spun into cloth; here is a handful of wheat ground, kneaded, baked, and set on the cloth.

2
REVERENCE
The Word Is Real

I was nineteen years old before it dawned on me that the Twenty-third Psalm was not written in English. Of course I had known for many years that the books my tradition called the Old Testament were written in Hebrew and the books we called the New Testament were written in Greek. But it wasn't until I was in college that a little window opened in my mind, and I suddenly encountered the fundamental otherness of my Bible's language. The psalmist was not a late-twentieth-century American. The psalmist was not a young girl lying on her rubber-lined mattress in a college dorm room, grieving the betrayal of a high school boyfriend and searching for some comfort among the words of a poem she had known since childhood.

You anoint my head with oil, the psalm declared, *my cup overflows.* Suddenly the Bible's foreignness overwhelmed me. The book I held in my hand had come to me down many twisting trails and through many transmogrifications of language. It was a miracle. It was an oracle. It was mine and not mine, all at once.

My realization that the psalm was written in an ancient tongue, I see now, *was* the comfort I was seeking. For when I tucked that suddenly strange text under my arm and walked outside with an inexplicable need to get moving, I felt the trees and the very sidewalks holding me up, felt them as created things that were a bodied part of God's tapestry, God's text. The language of the Bible was real. The sidewalks were real. My broken heart was real, but I had not fallen through the world. I didn't have to know why this had happened or how it fit into some larger cosmic plan. I just had to know that God's word and world were real.

This sense of the "realness" of the Bible, I've discovered, is fundamentally Jewish in nature. It's why Orthodox Jewish women still sometimes lean into the aisle to kiss the Torah scroll as it's carried to the front of the synagogue. It's why the first act of young boys beginning their studies in medieval yeshivas was to lick smeared honey off chalk slates inscribed with Bible verses. It's why the Torah is never thrown out or given away even when worn beyond repair, but rather is buried in a *genizah*, a special cemetery for scripture.

My family and the evangelical churches I grew up in put great emphasis on the Bible: its authority, its centrality. My parents joined our church not because the people were friendly or the sermons were good but because the congregation grounded its identity explicitly in the Bible. Each member of my family had his or her own Bible, given as a special birthday or Christmas gift, and we packed the small volumes in our suitcases for trips as automatically as we packed our underwear and toothbrushes.

Yet as much as we loved the Bible, we didn't sacralize it. Though we treated our leather-bound books with the utmost care, it would never have occurred to us to revere the physical text itself, to locate God's actual transforming presence in the crinkly pages, the twin columns of text, the word "In" which opens the first chapter of Genesis or the words "Hallelu Ya" that end the Psalms. It didn't matter to us whether we read the Bible in translation or in its original languages, read it together or alone, read it on the page or recited it from memory, read it with or without a ritual prayer.

When we read the Bible, we located God's power outside the words that named and described it. We called each piece of scripture a "passage," and our aim in reading it was precisely that: We passed through the words on the page to get to the spiritual truth to which they were pointing. I sometimes paused to marvel at the beauty or complexity or strangeness of a passage, but dwelling on such specifics of language always felt a little indulgent somehow, a distraction. My religious tradition was more about *movement*. The primary task of our Bible reading was traveling, through the trusted medium of Holy Scripture, toward a perfection of knowing and doing that was somewhere out there, beyond words.

The Jewish way of reading, I am learning, is less about progressing than about digging in, holding on—

Reverence: The Word Is Real

not passing through words but dwelling in them and on them, under and around them. Torah, like the ancient Temple, is a place to enter, experience, and revere. Holy words are things to be savored, and to study scripture is to digest the words into the body, like food. Jews in fact refer to each piece of scripture not as a "passage" but as a *parsha,* or "portion."

In Judaism, scripture is not a signpost pointing to truth but a portion of the truth itself—not just a promise to be fulfilled or a commandment to be obeyed, but a real-time serving of scriptural food to be tasted, chewed, and digested into the body, mind, heart, and soul.

The Bible is full of references to language as food. *When your words came, I ate them,* the prophet Jeremiah says to the God whose voice he hears. *Eat this scroll I am giving you and fill your stomach with it,* God says to the prophet Ezekiel, and to the nation of Israel entire: *Listen to me, and eat what is good, and your soul will delight in the richest of fare.* Much later, the Gospel writer John, ever seeking to connect Hebrew with Greek, Jewish with Christian, would call Jesus both the Word of God and the Bread of Life. "The scriptures teach us how to read the scriptures," says Biblical scholar Donald Akenson, and the verses quoted above seem to me now a wonderful set of clues about how to begin: to take God's words into our mouths with the same hunger and attention we bring to the food we eat.

TOWARD A PERSONAL PRACTICE

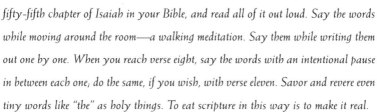

Mothers tell their children to chew their food slowly. It is good to approach scripture with a similar tactic: Find the fifty-fifth chapter of Isaiah in your Bible, and read all of it out loud. Say the words while moving around the room—a walking meditation. Say them while writing them out one by one. When you reach verse eight, say the words with an intentional pause in between each one; do the same, if you wish, with verse eleven. Savor and revere even tiny words like "the" as holy things. To eat scripture in this way is to make it real.

When in my twenties I fell in love with poetry, took out some big loans, packed up my small red Mazda hatchback with everything I owned and drove from Denver to New York to start graduate school, it never occurred to me that I was searching for a new way to read the Bible. I wanted language, and language alone. I wanted to bend grammar, curse freely, invite illogical leaps of association and unjustifiable juxtapositions to dine at my mental table, and none of that seemed compatible with my faith tradition. I was bowled over by the power of language in the novels and poems I was reading, but I had not yet recognized that such power might be rooted in, connected with, the God and the ancient scriptures I had studied in youth groups and college Bible studies.

It is not easy to write powerful words on one's own, I quickly discovered. I may have declared myself to be a writer, may have given up on evangelical religion and that early plan to go to Christian seminary, yet I found I could not so easily detach from my tradition's drive to pass through language toward an always intangible spiritual reality: Ideas had always mattered so much more than the words that conveyed them.

Now I wandered the campus at night, lonely, broke, staring up at the sky with what felt like a writerly intensity, muttering under my breath, "The moon! The moon!" I wanted to capture on paper the moon's very soul—but it took me a while to figure out that first I had to learn how to make a body of words that could house that soul. I had to learn that language, in the poet Mary Oliver's words, is "rich, and malleable. It is a living, vibrant material, and every part works in conjunction with every other part—the content, the pace, the diction, the rhythm, the tone—as well as the very sliding, floating, thumping, rapping sounds of it."

Slowly, I began to work with words. My thumbs turned gray from paging through *Merriam-Webster's Rhyming Dictionary* and *Roget's Thesaurus*. Those (still) lonely nights now found me muttering *satellite, luminary, Lurga the goddess . . . moonfaced, moonlighting, moonshine, moonstruck . . . monastery, money, monkey business, murk.* Each sound played out in my mouth and on the page; with words I fashioned bone, skin, sinew—and I could feel whole pages starting to move.

In my second year of graduate school, I met weekly with nine other students and a professor for a two-hour poetry workshop. We passed out copies of new poems to be critiqued, argued over, and sometimes praised. Buzzwords about language floated in the air: "fresh," "original," "haunting," "strange." One week a student scorched another student's poem because it used the word "butterfly." No one can use that word in a poem, he said; it's sentimental and clichéd.

There was a long pause. The teacher, a wonderful poet named Marie Howe, smiled slowly. "Please take out a piece of paper and write the following words," she said. "Butterfly, rainbow, flower, happiness. . ." We knew where she was headed, and as we scribbled someone cursed mildly under his breath, *oh Jesus*. "Jesus," Marie immediately said, adding the ultimate overused cliché to the list. Everyone laughed, and she gave the assignment: Write a poem of your own using at least two words on the list.

Oh joy. Oh hell. I'd been given just the challenge I needed: to apply my imagination and my poetic tools directly to the faith I'd been trying to ignore. I had distanced myself from an overt Christian identity, but somehow I couldn't choose as my subject anything other than the "J-word" throbbing at me from my notebook. Still, in that competitive, distinctly non-religious environment, no way was I going to offer up language that felt like a saccharine Christian psalm. I had to make a body of words about Jesus that would truly live and breathe there in that formidable Wednesday night gathering of writers.

Just a few months prior to this was when my summer writing teacher had challenged me to consider how

Jews read the Bible, and so I had begun to examine various Jewish approaches to holy language. I discovered the works of philosopher Abraham Joshua Heschel, for example, who wrote, "The word of God is not an object of contemplation, not an 'ought to,' an idea suspended between being and non-being. . . . [It is] a perpetual event, a demand of God more real than a mountain, more powerful than all thunders."

I had been used to thinking about the words of the Bible as *true*. Now I began to wonder, how was that different from thinking about them as *real?* And not just contemplating them, Heschel reminded me, but tangibly encountering them. Mountain. Thunder. Body. Bread. *When your words came, I ate them.*

All this was at work in my mind as I struggled to complete my assignment for the Wednesday workshop. I'd come across a poem by the French surrealist poet André Breton called "Freedom of Love" that described different parts of his wife's body—her hair, her teeth, her throat, her back—using wildly inventive metaphors. I decided to make a similar description of Jesus, and for a week I funneled my imagination into lists and lists of possible metaphors. Here is a part of the poem that emerged:

Jesus with the chest of a blossoming rosebush
Jesus with hips of a rollicking skiff
with thighs of rung crystal
and with calves of an ancient mooring
Jesus with eyes of wild oak and sung honey

The Burning Word

Jesus with eyes full of desert
Eyes full of mirror and a roaring horizon
Eyes of a bird beyond the gun.

At the time I was conscious only of wanting to write a poem that would impress my Wednesday night colleagues. But deeper down was the desire to find and take hold of that "realness" I'd once sensed in the Twenty-third Psalm. I didn't want to assert some absolute truth about my own religion. I just wanted to make the word "Jesus" viscerally felt to the poets sitting around that table, including me: to recover, using my imagination, some sense of what the poet Scott Cairns calls the "indeterminate enormity" contained in that name.

To make God's name, the definitive Word, *real* to its hearers—this desire lies at the heart of both Jewish and Christian traditions. The Jewish community makes it real by reverently refusing to fully spell out God's most intimate name, YHWH, or to ever speak it out loud. My Christian community makes it real by speaking all God's names enthusiastically (a poster listing every Biblical moniker for the Messiah in a rainbow cascade of fonts was hung somewhere on a wall in every church I attended as a child). The Talmud makes the words of Torah real by studying them, according their every syllable a God-intended significance. And Midrash makes the same words real by elaborating upon them, arguing with them, turning and turning them with the God-made engine of human imagination.

Reverence: The Word Is Real

Consider one name for God found in the Hebrew scriptures:
Elohim, meaning Our God of Creative Power. *Write*
out this name and spend a minute or two looking at it, attending to its every letter,
every sound. Then, with your pen in hand, quiet your mind and begin to write with-
out stopping: What response from you does this name call forth? If you wish, try this
exercise with additional names: El Shaddai (God Who is Sufficient), *El-Olam*
(God of Everlasting Time), *or others you might know.*

For me, the Jewish practice of dwelling on scripture as a "portion" has come to seem more real than the Greek-influenced Christian practice of moving through it as a "passage." Yet when I look again at the psalm that first woke me up to the power of the Bible's language, I am somehow not surprised that it contains both ideas: *He guides me in right paths,* the psalmist declares, and then later, *You spread a table before me.* Passage and portion, silence and speech, soul and body—no one of these, taken separately, can fully contain the power of God's word, or the shocking realness of his intent to offer it to us. We need them all.

Perhaps the best acknowledgment of this need is the Jewish *bar/bat mitzvah,* the ritual reading of scripture that every observant Jew formally undertakes as an adolescent. For many months before their thirteenth birthday, young Jews of every stripe, Orthodox or Reform or

Conservative, must choose a portion of Torah, study it, digest it, and learn how to pronounce it and write it in Hebrew, the original tongue by which it was given to Moses and to Israel. Then in a public and highly celebrated ceremony, each young person declaims this scripture out loud in the synagogue and offers his or her own interpretation of its meaning.

The *bar/bat mitzvah* is a major rite of passage—a sacred, concretely experienced passing through from childhood to adulthood. It has become my conviction that the spiritual, redemptive passage Christianity aims for is ultimately not achievable without engaging with the here and now as a portion of God's full revelation to humanity. Getting to the true, in other words, is not possible without deeply encountering the real.

Torah offers very specific instructions about how to do this: "Now what I am commanding you today is not too difficult for you or beyond your reach. . . . No, the Word is very near you; it is in your mouth and in your heart so you may obey it." "Fix these words of mine in your hearts and minds; tie them as symbols on your hands and bind them on your foreheads."

Stringing words together into poems or stories or sermons is one way of living out those instructions. Packing a dog-eared Bible in your suitcase on every trip you take is another way. The Talmud offers yet another way, urging every Jew to write out the entire Torah once in the course of a lifetime, to physically feel beneath the fingers that sacred text, that "perpetual event," that "demand . . . more real than a mountain"

Reverence: The Word Is Real

that is the word of God. This is not simply a mundane copy job—just as my piece about Jesus' body was not simply a repetitive description, nor was my encounter with Psalm Twenty-three simply reading out loud.

Such encounters with the Bible are holy events. They are acts of reverence that honor the Bible by simultaneously claiming it as our own, and confessing that it can never be owned by us or nailed down by our particular faith tradition. They acknowledge God's word as pure gift: ours and not ours, all at once.

TOWARD A PERSONAL PRACTICE

Pick up a Bible and hold it in your hands. Open the front pages and read the tiny notes explaining how the Hebrew and Greek Scriptures were translated into English. Think about the long history of how these words came to rest in your hands. In what ways is this holy book yours and not yours, all at once—the way only a gift can be? In what ways can you revere this gift? In what ways can you honor it as real?

3
CURIOSITY
The Word Is Burning

*I*n my reading of Midrash and other rabbinic literature, the name of Moses appears again and again. "From the mouth of God to the hand of Moses," Jewish congregations proclaim, every time Torah is read out loud in a synagogue. Moses saw God in all God's glory, yet amazingly, he did not die. He walked and talked with God on the mountain of Sinai; when he came down his face glowed with inner fire, and he carried the Ten Commandments, the first written words of YHWH, in his arms.

Jewish tradition teaches that in his head the prophet Moses carried much more than could be inscribed on two stone tablets—that during their mountaintop meetings God dictated to Moses the entire Torah, not just the books of Genesis, Exodus, Deuteronomy, Leviticus, and Numbers, but also every word of commentary about those books that rabbis have generated down through the ages. Thus Moses is revered among rabbinic Jews as "Moshe Rabbenu," the master teacher. Yet at the beginning, when he first encountered God's voice, he wasn't master or teacher of anything—he was simply curious:

> Now Moses, tending the flock of his father-in-law Jethro, the priest of Midian, drove the flock into the wilderness, and came to Horeb, the mountain of God. An angel of the LORD appeared to him in a blazing fire out of a bush. He gazed, and there was a bush all aflame, yet the bush was not consumed. Moses said, "I must turn aside to look at this marvelous sight; why doesn't the bush burn up?" When the LORD saw that he had turned aside to look, God called to him out of the bush: "Moses! Moses!" He answered, "Here I am." And He said, "Do not come closer. Remove your sandals from your feet, for the place on which you stand is holy ground. I am," He said, "the God of your father, the God of Abraham, the God of Isaac, and the God of Jacob." And Moses hid his face, for he was afraid to look at God.

A nudge of curiosity, a startled turn of the head: Moses' intimacy with God begins with a classic double take. *Why doesn't that bush burn up?* He takes a step closer to investigate—and hears his own name being called out from the flame. Now suddenly the frank gaze of a curious mind becomes a terrifying glimpse into the face of the One True God, and Moses quickly and rightly hides his head. Yet there he is, on holy ground with the God of his fathers, and an intimate, difficult, exhilarating relationship has begun.

The Burning Word

When I look closely at this story, trying to read it the way a rabbi might read, I notice that it's only after Moses stops to investigate the curious bush that God calls out his name. Why does God need to see that initial sign of human interest before he can declare his own? Does God hide and wait because, like a shy new friend or lover, he fears rejection? Or does God hide and wait because he fears overwhelming the human Moses, killing him just by his mere presence?

"Perhaps that is the meaning of the burning bush," says Abraham Joshua Heschel. "Namely, that to reveal He must conceal, that to impart His wisdom He must hide His power." In his actions and in his words God continually holds out revelation, holds out wisdom, but it is hidden, and we must seek it out. *If you seek me, you will ever surely find me*, says the Lord. *I will be found by you.*

Moses had the burning bush; we have the Bible. This is the conviction that lies behind the whole enterprise of midrash. If I want to come close to the God of the Bible, to step onto the holy ground of his presence, then I must wake up my curiosity and look for God in the strange, hidden, and burning places of scripture. Curiosity is the starting point of midrash—and the question is the first tool midrash employs in every encounter with the Bible. Questions lead us deeper into the text, into the smoldering gaps and silences where YHWH dwells.

These "hidden spaces" of scripture open up whenever we encounter pronouncements that trouble us, details that refuse to fall into our sense of a logical pattern, or language that sparks a question in us, often mundane, sometimes profound, sometimes desperate. In my own experience, the Bible is full of language that pulls me up short, makes me cringe, or simply strikes me dumb with confusion. But whereas Midrash calls the reader to stare straight into the dark holes of scripture, and to use curiosity and questions to dig even deeper into those holes, my own tradition's way of reading has often seemed to do just the opposite.

I remember encountering passages of scripture in a student-led college study that stumped everyone in the room, that clashed head-on with our developing cultural norms. The first chapter of Saint Paul's letter to the Romans, for example, condemning heathens and homosexuals. The verses in both Hebrew and Greek Scriptures calling for the silence and servitude of women in church and in marriage. The God-sanctioned slaughter of Egyptians, Canaanites, and disobedient Israelites in the Hebraic histories and prophecies, and the bloody segregation of sinners and saved in the Christian book of Revelation.

Fierce questions arose in our discussions of these passages, and frustrating arguments divided our group so deeply that the leader finally declared a moratorium on questions and moved us to scriptures that were easier to understand—interpretations that were easier to agree upon.

I wish now we had recognized that in the midst of those arguments we were on holy ground. Painful though it was to ask questions of scripture and not find answers that satisfied us, it would have helped to ponder the fact that it was the text itself that raised them, that by its very difficulty the text was calling out to us. God was calling to us through each syllable of these troubling words, inviting us to turn them in our hearts and minds and mouths, and to be turned by them, mysteriously and uncomfortably, toward God.

TOWARD A PERSONAL PRACTICE

Find Exodus 32:19–29 in your Bible, and read it out loud. How might God be hiding in these difficult words? Whether or not you can make sense of them, can you sit with this text as a holy thing? Can you conceive of conversation with this text, however troubled, as a holy exchange?

The best way I know to explain how curiosity can pull us onto holy ground is to tell a story about a difficult question put to me by my high school boyfriend in Littleton, Colorado, one year on the fourth of July. We were standing in line at a party buffet before the fireworks; I had turned sixteen that March. As we spooned chunks of potato salad onto our plates, I mentioned offhandedly that my parents' anniversary was two weeks away. "What year were they married?" my boyfriend asked. When I told him, he said, "Hm," and then: "How come your birthday is only seven months after their wedding day?"

It was a question that had never occurred to me—and it shook me up a bit. Though they themselves had never made pronouncements about sex before marriage being wrong, the church tradition they'd chosen to raise me in certainly had, vigorously and frequently. Now the mild curiosity of a math-oriented teenaged boy had called that teaching—and my parents' own moral integrity—into question. Like fingers gliding along a wall and suddenly tracing the clean outlines of a door, the prosaic question "how come?" had exposed a hidden space in my life I didn't know existed.

The next day I walked through that new door. With a curiosity still only slightly sharper than that of the boy who'd posed it, I took the question to my parents— in the middle of a restaurant meal, as I recall. They were gracious in their response. They shared with me, awkwardly but openly, a very private part of their history, and as the conversation unfolded, larger questions emerged in me.

Why had they taught me that sex outside of marriage is wrong if they had done it themselves? And how could it be so wrong if . . . would I even exist if they had kept God's . . . and suddenly I was overwhelmed by the implications. A little earthquake was roughing up my otherwise smooth inner landscape; I found myself barely standing on rather terrifying holy ground. God was suddenly bigger, much bigger than my adolescent self had imagined Him to be, and the easy church mathematical equations of sin and consequence suddenly became more complex.

It is possible to equate questioning with challenge, suspicion, interrogation, demand. We tend to value answers more highly than questions, as the goal worth achieving, as the finish line. Midrash, however, equates questions with intimacy. Midrash values the question, and the sacred language that gives rise to it, as ground for meeting with God. When my three-year-old son, Aidan, asks "why?" about everything from brushing his teeth to the shape of bananas, I understand, dimly, that it's not explanation he wants so much as closeness. When my parents chose to walk with me through the door of my uncomfortable question, we didn't find answers, clarification, or resolution. Instead we found intimacy—an intimacy borne out of a mutual willingness to seek out the hidden places, to come closer to the burning bush, to question the received text of our separate and joined lives.

TOWARD A PERSONAL PRACTICE

Take some time to think about the extent to which you welcome questions, and the extent to which you fear them: in your relationship with God; with the Bible; with the various communities to which you belong. What might happen in these relationships if you were to actively regard questions as opportunities for increased intimacy?

Of course, closeness between parents and children is distinctly different from closeness between God and humans. I may have grown up picturing God as a loving father and Jesus as a loving friend—but these images

Curiosity: The Word Is Burning

are hard to maintain when ranged against the Bible's frequent and fearsome pictures of God as destroyer, avenger, and punisher, or Jesus as thundering prophet, brash upstart, cryptic naysayer, and ultimate judge.

An encounter with the God of the Bible, therefore, should not be sought lightly. As Moses knows when he hides his face, as Israel's ancient priests knew when they tied a safety rope around an ankle before entering the inner sanctum of the Temple called the Holy of Holies, to come into the presence of the Most High God is to put one's life in peril.

The language of the Bible, thankfully, offers us some protection from God's power. Mystical Judaism claims that Torah existed before the creation of the world, and describes its script as "white fire engraved with black fire." Like the burning bush in the wilderness, the letters on the paper are on fire, but they are not consumed. The more closely we examine that burning bush, the Bible, the more steps we take onto the holy ground where a powerful God waits to speak with us. Biblical language, like the burning bush, can hold the presence of God and not be consumed. We can't look the Creator of the universe in the face or we'll die, but we can look at holy language, not die, and see something of God.

"The cry of the Israelites has reached me," God says to Moses, "and I have seen the way the Egyptians are oppressing them. So now, go. I am sending you to Pharaoh to bring my people the Israelites out of Egypt." Moses' story reveals to us that God has his own curiosities and imaginings, and while they are wholly good,

they are generally not benign. Moses is not killed out-
right in his meeting with God, but when he emerges
from the encounter, his life is set on a path of risk and
responsibility that will take him back to Egypt, back to
the desert, and right to the brink of, but not into, the
Promised Land. Our purpose in reading Holy Scripture
is to meet God, meet ourselves, learn how to live. God
purposes much more: He wants to use us to redeem the
world.

We are not used to contemplating an all-knowing
God as one who is curious. But it is God who imagines
freedom for us all, God whose faithful curiosity about
the future of the world has set the text of the Bible
eternally on fire. The amazing journey of Moses and the
nation of Israel has for thousands of years inspired all
kinds of new journeys toward freedom in the world.
When inspired leaders rise up among us and call out new
visions of justice and peace, what we hear is really an
echo, still resounding, of God's most ancient yearnings.

TOWARD A PERSONAL PRACTICE

*Consider this paraphrase of Hebrews 11:40, translated by
Eugene Peterson: "God had a better plan for us: that their
faith and our faith would come together to make one completed whole, their lives of
faith not complete apart from ours." Jewish tradition holds that our own imaginative
grappling with scripture is the most important way such wholeness can come about.*

Find the burning words of Isaiah 6:1-8 in a Bible. Read them out loud. Put the Bible down, and find your own way to say to God, "Here I am." Consider taking off your shoes! If you can, try doing this exercise with a friend or group, changing "I am" to "we are."

The Bible records that at the end of his long life Moses angered God, who declared that he would not allow the prophet to enter into the promised land he had spent forty years toiling toward. Instead, just at the border of the land of milk and honey, Moses dies. Midrashic literature is fascinated by the seeming rupture of a relationship considered in Judaism to be more intimate than any other in history. One legend says that when the great prophet dies he is taken up to heaven. There he sees God in his study, hunched over a table with a Torah scroll spread open upon it. God is using inks and brushes to add all kinds of dots and ornaments to the text.

"Why are you doing that?" Moses asks, ever daring to give voice to his curiosity. Without looking up from his work God tells him, "In the future a rabbi named Akiva will arise who is so brilliant he can fathom every mystery of the Torah. I am making his job harder for him!"

"What do you mean?" Moses asks, and for answer he is immediately transported forward in time to a classroom where Rabbi Akiva is teaching on Torah. Moses, standing in the back of the classroom, is bewildered: He doesn't understand a word the sage is saying. Then a student raises his hand and asks, "Where does that teaching come from, rabbi?" Rabbi Akiva replies, "It comes from Moshe Rabbenu, the master teacher." Immediately Moses is transported back to the study room where God is still working.

It is strange to contemplate that this man who carries everything ever said about Torah in his head still has questions, remains bewildered. But clearly, God is no longer hiding from him. If he seems indifferent, he also seems *present.* Perhaps one lesson we draw from this story is that no matter how close we feel to God, no matter how much knowledge we may have mastered, the questions never end. Another lesson is that God is not so much hiding *from* us as he is hiding *for* us. He is purposefully creating the places where, with curiosity and perseverance, we can find him.

The Jewish tradition deliberately encourages its youth to develop such an attitude of fearless seeking, through midrashic texts like the annual Passover haggadah. During the ritual seder meal, each child in a family is obliged to ask four traditional questions, after being told that there are four possible attitudes to take: that of the wise son, who knows the question and asks it; that of the wicked son, who knows the question but refuses to ask it; that of the simple son, who knows the question but is indifferent to it; and that of the ignorant son, who does not know the question and therefore is unable to ask. Though the Passover ceremony contains the answers to the four traditional questions, the emphasis is on seeking rather than finding. The definitive, celebrated beginning

Curiosity: The Word Is Burning

of a Jewish child's religious life is not the first expression of belief but the first genuinely expressed question.

To practice Midrash is to search out the questions, all of them, knowing that at any point our questions may pull us into the place where divine mystery dwells. I am learning that the ground of scripture is our ground, and at the same time it is holy ground. We are invited by God to till its soil, though we do so at the risk of being changed, and of being charged. Midrash requires both the reverence that causes Moses to hide his face, and the chutzpah that frees him to ask everything of God, even as God asks everything of him.

4
COMMUNITY
To Argue Is To Love

*T*he word is real. The word is burning. In the Jewish view, Torah is far too hot to handle on one's own. "Make for yourself a teacher," says the oldest tractate of the Talmud. "Acquire for yourself a friend. And give everyone the benefit of the doubt."

To the ancient rabbis, and to many practicing Jews today, studying the Bible is a distinctly communal activity. As young children in yeshiva, observant Jews are paired off into *hevrutot,* or study friends, and as adults, years later, they gather in the *bet midrash,* or study house, in a group of ten or twenty or a hundred to hunch in pairs over open Bibles, perhaps with the same partner they've had since youth. (The *hevruta* relationship is so significant that the Israeli Army takes pains to assign childhood *hevrutot* to serve in the same combat units.)

A teacher announces the appointed Torah portion, but does not interpret it or even read it. Instead, all over the room, one *hevruta* begins to read the assigned section out loud. The other half of each pair listens intently (one would have to, with so many voices raised in the room), then jumps in with a response, thus commencing an intense, often hours-long session of questioning, answering, arguing—a robust, communal exploration of a text which, tradition holds, God commands them to interpret.

In Judaism, intimacy cannot be separated from argument, nor can reading or study be separated from community. I have suggested in an earlier chapter that "conversation" is a good descriptor for the way Midrash approaches the Bible. Yet the casual, unattached encounter we usually associate with that word is a far cry from the hectic intensity of a *bet midrash*, where all over the room heads are vigorously nodding and hands are slicing the air to emphasize a point, flipping knowingly through pages of heavy volumes to find prooftexts located all through Torah and the Talmud. This is high stakes conversation—where not just the text on the table but also the multiple arguments over what it means are considered sacred, vital to the religious life of everyone in the room, of the entire community, and of the entire nation of Israel.

This intense communal conversation, anchored in Torah, isn't bounded by time or space. It spreads across generations, ethnicities, and languages: The dialogue between two *hevrutot* is mirrored on the page in front of them in blocks of Hebrew text arranged around each portion of Scripture, presenting commentary by rabbis from many different centuries.

The Rabbinic Bible, first published in 1516 by the Christian printer Daniel Bomberg, gives physical shape to a huge unfolding conversation across ages and continents. Along with the Talmud and other Jewish texts that follow a similar layout, the Rabbinic Bible has been called society's first "hypertext," preceding by five hundred years the efficiency and fluidity of today's Internet Web page.

Thus Jewish readers in today's *bet midrash* are arguing not only with each other but with Rashi, the great French interpreter of the eleventh century, with Ibn Ezra of the twelfth century, with Nahmanides of the thirteenth century, and with others—as many as can be arranged on the page. The text of this commentary frequently reads like dialogue in a play: "Rabbi Eliezer said . . ." "Rabbi Akiva said . . ." These figures become so familiar to students of Jewish literature that nicknames, jokes, and supernatural legends get mixed in with the historical conversation.

Strikingly, the coherence of this vast historical and contemporary Jewish textual conversation in no way depends on the resolution of so many differing opinions. On the contrary, Jews accept as a given the impossibility of finding clear answers to the troubling questions sparked by the Scriptures. "When the Torah was given at Sinai," says the Talmud, "it came with thirteen methods of interpretation, and forty-nine arguments proving that each item is correct and forty-nine arguments proving that it is not." These arguments and more have been carefully recorded down through the ages, but the Talmud rarely if ever declares one interpretation the *right* one. "They lie there next to each other on the same page," says Jewish scholar David Stern, "awaiting the reader who will study them all, gleaning each writing for its own contribution and added significance."

TOWARD A PERSONAL PRACTICE

Gather three books that have been significant to your life and set them in front of you. One of them could even be a book from the Bible. Think about when each was written, and think about the connections that might be made among them. What would it be like to take part in a roundtable conversation with the authors of these books? What questions or arguments would you contribute?

If most of the books you read were written fairly recently, consider branching out to books written in previous centuries or millennia. Consciously expand your sense of being connected through your reading to the whole human community of questioners and seekers.

The Jewish study tradition's astonishing mix of intimacy, argument, and time can be captured perfectly with one image: family. Where else do we find such intense communion across generations with people who can vehemently disagree with us? Though as a child my own church tradition did not view community or argument as necessary to a rich encounter with the Bible, when I came to learn about Midrash I was reminded of the dynamics of my relationship with my own father—in particular, two conversations in my adolescence that, I see now, significantly shaped my approach to scripture study.

The Burning Word

The first, when I was twelve, centered on one of my Sunday school teacher's troubling statements about what women could and could not do in church. How can that be right? I asked my dad, and he said, your teachers have much to give you, and you should always take seriously what they say. But ultimately you must weigh what you are taught against what you yourself, based on your own studies, know to be true. Then you must set aside those teachings you deem to be false or misguided.

43

I was a little shocked at the permission he was giving me, but his words rang true. I got my Bible and found the texts my teacher had quoted about the proper roles of women in the church. I was twelve, and on my own, but in my unsophisticated way I embarked on my first real conversation with scripture, and by this I mean: I brought my own mind and morals and imagination to bear upon a portion of a text that deeply troubled me, yet that I believed to be God-inspired. In the end, I thoughtfully rejected my Sunday school teacher's declarations.

I wish I could say I talked to him about my conclusions face to face; I did not. I wish I could say my father and I and my teacher sat down together with Bibles in our laps and continued the argument. We did not— communal disagreement and dialogue just weren't things my church understood to be valuable to religious life.

Still, in the intimacy and privacy of our family, my father had urged me to develop my own judgment. The test of this new freedom came a year or so later, when in a friendly discussion I found myself disagreeing, out loud, for the first time, with Dad himself. After a moment of surprised silence, he began to explore my rebuttal, actively encouraging my adolescent reasoning without in any way ceding his own right to free judgment. In many conversations since then we have carved out between us an arena of intimate theological, intellectual, and political wrangling that in many ways resembles the passionate back-and-forth of a Jewish *bet midrash*.

In my experience, such free and intimate argument with someone who holds profoundly different views is a rare and precious experience. I imagine that when my father's time comes to pass on from this earth, I will feel something akin to what the ancient sage in the following Talmud story feels:

> . . . And Resh Lakish died. And Rebbe Yochanan suffered his loss greatly. The Rabbis said, "Who do we have that can help settle his mind? Let us bring him Eliezer ben Padat, for he is sharp in his learning." Eliezer ben Padat went and sat before Yochanan and for everything Yochanan said, Eliezer ben Padat brought a text to support Yochanan's argument. Rebbe Yochanan said, "You're not like Resh Lakish. When I said something in front of him, he would challenge me with twenty-four questions which I would have to answer, and from that the Torah would be richer—and you, you just support me! So, I have no way of knowing

whether what I'm saying is right!" Yochanan then ripped his cloak and wailed, "Where are you son of Lakish, where are you?"

TOWARD A PERSONAL PRACTICE

The rabbi in the story above claims that "the Torah is richer" because of his friend's challenges and arguments. Does this mean that the rabbi's personal understanding is richer—or does it mean that the actual Scriptures are richer, deepened and fulfilled in a way they would not be if these two companions were not arguing over each verse?

Find a hevruta—*someone who will sit down with you and discuss this question. Read the Resh Lakish/Rebbe Yochanan story together—or, if you prefer, another Jewish story from this book. Take turns reacting to the words, formulating questions, etc. Keep the conversation going.*

Passion is a key ingredient of Jewish reading. Debate and discussion would not be so treasured in the Talmudic and Midrashic traditions if the opinions held by the sages were not held fiercely. Love would not be love without passion, after all, and neither would argument. The classic illustration of this zeal is the story of Rabbi Eliezar and the Sages, who debate to an extreme degree whether or not, according to scripture, a clay oven that has shattered and been repaired can be accepted as ritually pure:

It has been taught: On that day Rabbi Eliezar brought forward every imaginable argument, but they did not accept them. Said he to them: "If the [law] agrees with me, let this carob-tree prove it!" Thereupon the carob-tree was torn a hundred cubits out of its place.

"No proof can be brought from a carob-tree," they retorted. Again he said to them: "If the [law] agrees with me, let the stream of water prove it!" Whereupon the stream of water flowed backwards.

"No proof can be brought from a stream of water," they rejoined.

Again he said to them: "If the [law] agrees with me, let it be proved from Heaven!" Whereupon a heavenly Voice cried out: "Why do you dispute with Rabbi Eliezar, seeing that in all matters the [law] agrees with him?!" But Rabbi Joshua arose and exclaimed: "It is not in heaven!" (Deut. 30.12).

What did he mean by this? Said Rabbi Jeremiah: "That the Torah had already been given at Mount Sinai; we pay no attention to a Heavenly Voice, because Thou hast long since written in the Torah at Mount Sinai, "After the majority must one incline" (Ex. 23.2).

Rabbi Nathan met Elijah [the prophet] and asked him: "What did the Holy One, Blessed be He, do in that hour?" "He laughed [with joy]," he replied, saying, 'My sons have defeated Me, My sons have defeated Me!'"

The Burning Word

Of the many Jewish stories I've encountered, this strange tale is my favorite. It is at once ridiculous and profound, individual and communal, audacious and reverent. The rabbis use nature, scripture quotations—called "prooftexts" in Judaism—and direct appeals to the Holy One to dispute their convictions about the law. The very cosmos seems to hinge on this argument about the purity of a clay oven!

And yet, despite the passion and conviction of every voice involved in the conversation—including God's—no clear answer is given to the original question: Is the repaired oven pure and acceptable or not? Contrary to a common perception among Christians, the Judaism that emerged around the Talmud and the Midrash really isn't concerned about the bottom line of the law. Ultimately, from a Jewish perspective, it may be more important to be in conversation with each other and get it "wrong," then to get it "right" but have the conversation stop.

As the story of Eliezar and the Sages suggests, however, this ongoing conversation about scripture is anything but casual. It recognizes and depends upon each one of us speaking truthfully from our *svara*, or gut—the seat of our most passionate, learned, and lived out convictions. At the same time, *svara* conversation assumes a deep level of humility, a clear understanding that each argument comes through and from a limited, flawed human being.

These are startling ideas to me, for I come from a tradition that seeks and articulates truths we can call certain, fixed, indisputable. Community, in this tradition, was defined more by mutual adherence to the same beliefs; communal conversation about scripture aimed to arrive at conclusions on which everyone agreed.

The churches I was raised in tended to be uncomfortable with arguments that lacked resolution—and in fact many of the Christian Bible's statements about argument are quite negative. The apostle Paul warns against "foolish controversies and genealogies and arguments and quarrels about the law, because these are unprofitable and useless," and Jesus himself is declared to fulfill the Isaiah description of the Messiah as one who "will not quarrel or cry out; no one will hear his voice in the streets."

Yet when I go back and try reading the Gospels with Jewish eyes, I see dramatic confrontations everywhere—between Jesus and the ruling teachers, between Jesus and his family, between Jesus and his closest friends.

TOWARD A PERSONAL PRACTICE

Read the twelfth chapter of Matthew in the Christian Bible.

Try to picture yourself there, as a Jew in a Jewish community. As honestly as possible, ask yourself: How would you respond to Jesus' words? You may find you have several quite conflicting emotional and intellectual reactions. If you can, study the passage again and engage your conflicts with a friend or small group. If you can, find someone of the Jewish faith and study the passage with them.

The Jewish tradition suggests that God relishes our arguments and shocking conjectures as much as my father relished my bold thirteen-year-old suppositions—that God observes our passionate dickering over his text with the same mixture of sober questioning, zesty humor, and finally undisguised admiration that ends the Talmud story with the joyful exclamation: "My sons have defeated Me! My sons have defeated Me!"

Dangerous as argument may be, with its potential for division, anger, heresy, and strife, I can't help considering that argument is, at its heart, a quest for love, for intimate connection to the Creator and to the human community we were created to be. "Where are you?" wails Rebbe Yochanan at the loss of his *hevruta*. Where are you?

TOWARD A PERSONAL PRACTICE

Read Psalm 133 out loud: "How good and pleasant it is when brothers live together in unity!" Does your picture of unity make space for argument? How can you expand that space in your own relationships, give it the buoyant joy that this psalm exudes?

5
SUFFERING
The Yeast of Exile

My husband and I share a joke between us, one of those moments in a marriage with roots of pain and eventual blossoms of laughter. Soon after our first child was born, we left the supportive New York community where we'd met, and moved to Savannah, Georgia, where we knew no one. On the drive south my husband mused happily about the job that awaited him. When he announced that he'd figured out his office e-mail address, fears about my own new job as full-time mother and homemaker suddenly loomed. "What will *my* address be?" I asked, and with a chuckle he said, "Judithkunst@nowheresville.com."

Nowheresville. It was meant as a joke, but the word ignited all my fears. I'd been a teacher, the center of daily attention in a classroom; I'd been a published poet and the editor of a scholarly journal. Now I'd be a mom in a town where nobody knew me. Now I'd be a housecleaner and cook, roles my string of room-and-board-included jobs had not prepared me for. In one stroke the cozy life I'd pictured snuggling with my son morphed into a threatening stretch of nothingness populated only by strip malls and lonely housewives.

In many ways, "nowheresville" turned out to be an accurate address, and the fears it triggered in me were not unwarranted—this new life would be harder than any I'd lived before. Yet eventually I would come to see that in fact my husband had given me exactly what I needed: a word to mark the precise intersection between my loss and as yet unrealized gain, a word that was at once *nowhere* and *now here.*

I didn't see the hope in this dismal word until, like the rabbis of old, I started studying it. When I did, nowheresville became now, here—two words rather than one, positive rather than negative, abundance rather than scarcity. With time, I found I was reading my life like a rabbi making midrash, allowing my own imagination to interact with and expand the given word, the given circumstance.

Among the most bewildering tasks of my new life in this new place was learning to cook. Throughout my twenties I had given more thought to how best to read a book while eating than to any other aspect of a meal. Now the kitchen was the center of my world, and it felt more like the Bermuda Triangle than the warm hearth featured in the novels on my shelves. I tried at first to cook what I was used to eating in restaurants, using recipes clipped from *Gourmet* magazine. But these complicated dishes were too expensive; my menus were a daily seesaw between Asian chicken-chestnut skewers and three-for-a-dollar boxes of macaroni and cheese.

Then an advertisement for The Good Cook's Book Club arrived in the mail. I joined, and soon *The Joy of Cooking* appeared on my doorstep, followed by other classic tomes. These books became my teachers, and slowly I learned how to make the basic elements of oil, salt, sugar, and spice react and interact with plants from the ground, meat from the field, heat from the stove I was beginning to love. This new world, the kitchen, felt both narrow and infinitely wide. I was focused on what was in front of me: stove, knife, mixing bowl—and I was beginning to see what riches can be found at the point where nowhere meets the here and now.

Narrow, yet infinitely wide; confined, yet curiously free—this is the paradox that can be found at the suffering heart of exile. I used to think that imagination was a fanciful thing, a gratuitous appendage useful only to artists and inventors. But when you find yourself suddenly torn from your familiar world and thrust into a new place where nothing can be taken for granted, where everything must be remade, then you realize that imagination is an essential tool for survival.

The history of the Jewish people bears this out. Conquered successively over centuries by Egypt, Babylon, and Rome, ancient Israel was repeatedly exiled, enduring such sufferings as slave labor, Temple desecration, infanticide, crippling taxation, corrupt puppet leaders, forced idol worship, and more. In each period of exile, Jewish prophets, poets, and priests

Suffering: The Yeast of Exile

poured the suffering of their people into language of piercing sorrow and astonishing beauty. The poems of grief and hope found in the Torah, in the Psalms and the book of Lamentations, and later in the Talmud, the Midrash, and the mystical texts of Kabbalah and Hasidism—these profound works represent the simmering interaction of exile, language, imagination, and Torah.

I recall as a child feeling mostly pity for the Jews, a people who seemed stuck, to my fuzzy perception, in a permanent state of exile. But now I am amazed by the Hebrew *response* to suffering: not the silence of despair, but rather a vast creative literature that, like the Torah it springs from, spans every emotion from joy to despair to persistent hope. Confined again and again to the hot kitchen of exile, Jewish writers from every age have turned to language—their mixing bowl, their knife— and from words made food to sustain them.

Reading the short book of Lamentations in the Bible is a simple way to see this creative response at work. In this outpouring of grief after the Babylonian destruction of Jerusalem, the book's author does not ramble and moan incoherently, as one might expect of a firsthand witness to great suffering. On the contrary, the first four chapters of this book-length poem follow a strict "recipe": Each line begins with a succeeding letter of the Hebrew alphabet. This structure becomes a kind of container for pain that the heart and mind cannot by themselves hold. By focusing intently on language—the same way I focused on my kitchen stove—the writer of

The Burning Word

Lamentations taps into an inventive energy that helps him survive his despair.

In the third chapter the lamenting poet leans on language even more, for this time each letter of the alphabet is repeated at the beginning of *three* lines before passing to the next letter. The tighter structure requires more from his imagination because his suffering is greater—the writer has moved from describing the invasion of Jerusalem from a distance to describing his own personal experience of it. "I am the man," the chapter begins, "who has seen affliction under the rod of [God's] wrath; he has driven me and brought me into darkness without any light." The increased difficulty in manipulating the language mirrors and contains the increased anguish of a man who feels punished and abandoned by God—and who suspects, moreover, that *his* actions have caused God's anger.

This painful kneading of words and grief binds the poet to his despair, and at the same time pushes him through it, toward hope, until eventually the Lamentations writer who declared that God is "like an enemy," finds himself proclaiming that "the steadfast love of the Lord never ceases, his mercies never come to an end." Finally, after chapter three, the tension eases a bit: Chapter four returns to the simple alphabet structure, and the fifth chapter sheds the "recipe" entirely in favor of a quiet, simple prayer.

"The LORD is my portion," says the writer of Lamentations, "therefore I will hope in him." The Lord is the giver of the word, and also the word given. In this painful, beautiful book, the nowheresville of exile has become the now, here of acceptance and hope.

TOWARD A PERSONAL PRACTICE

When have you seen suffering trigger or bring out a creative response? Find the short book of Lamentations in a Bible and read it out loud. Notice how the feelings of the speaker change from beginning to end.

Consider reading Lamentations again as your own creative response to another person's or community's suffering: Read it in conjunction with an open newspaper, or while watching a news program—mute the TV during commercials and read the Scriptures out loud.

In the lonely exile of my kitchen in Savannah, Georgia, I learned quickly how to follow a recipe, stick to a budget, and feed my family. But I don't think I became a real cook until I made my first pizza crust from scratch.

The simplicity of the ingredients surprised me: flour, oil, yeast, a little sugar, some hot water. I worked the ingredients into a dough, then let the yeast take over and work its own magic. Soon I was at work again, punching down the puffy ball of risen dough and prodding it with my thumbs into the wide circle of the pizza pan. Then the yeast went to work once more, rising to its final form in a five-hundred-degree oven.

The Burning Word

When I thought about it, I realized I was not just following a recipe here, going from point A to point B to achieve a specific outcome. I was entering a conversation. I wasn't using food, or making food, I was cooking *with* food. I didn't truly become a cook until I saw that I myself was one of the ingredients. Then everything about the work became a joy.

Jews have always claimed conversation—with God and with each other—as their primary mode of language. It is frequently painful, filled with questions and accusations on both sides, but it is a conversation that never ends, and it is anchored, always, in Torah. Like the yeast in my pizza dough, the Jewish imagination works and reworks its sacred texts, and in the heat of suffering, new words rise. It is not the fanciful imagining of "making something up" that produces these new words; rather it is the formidable innovation of making do, of drawing from something already present, something eternally new.

Though the word "midrash" actually appears twice in the Hebrew Bible, once in the second book of Kings and once in the first book of Chronicles, the use of the term to describe the uniquely playful, imaginative response to scripture did not emerge until after the *second* destruction of Jerusalem, this time by Roman troops. It was in the aftermath of this second tragic annihilation that the flowering of Midrash came into full creative bloom, as exiled rabbis sought to make sense of an intensity of suffering that had not been seen since the Babylonian exile.

Suffering: The Yeast of Exile

Here again Jews found themselves at that same mysterious intersection of loss and gain, exile and imagination. Here again they find themselves in nowheresville. And now instead of inventing poetic structures to follow as recipes, they invented stories, analogies, parables, and dialogues of such vitality that centuries later they are as sacred and useful to contemporary Jews as the holy words of Torah.

It remains amazing to me that these rabbis did not turn away from the old scriptures that described Israel's earlier struggles and sufferings; on the contrary, they took them as the given word, the foundation for their own new struggles. "Turn it and turn it again," they insisted, "for everything is contained therein."

The first recorded midrashic conversations adhered very closely, yet very creatively, to specific books of the Bible. One collection of Midrashim is called *Genesis Rabbah*, another *Leviticus Rabbah*, and yet another *Lamentations Rabbah*. Verse by verse, the rabbis—some named and some anonymous—puzzled at and worked over the holy texts of ancient Israel. And in that creative work, that "cooking," the rabbis found new ways to make sense of their own, contemporary suffering.

TOWARD A PERSONAL PRACTICE

A simple way to begin "cooking" with the raw ingredients of scripture is to rewrite a psalm using your own words. Read and copy out Psalm 42, for example, replacing any specific names or ancient images with terms and pictures more evocative of your own era and experience.

The Burning Word

Though it was often lonely work, the cooking I did in Savannah did not take place in isolation: It took place in the context of a marriage. The imagination and attention I gave to the word "nowheresville" was colored always by the knowledge that my husband had given me that name. I had to reconcile myself, therefore, not just to the name but also to its author. Jews face the same task, for they too are in a relationship; they too must reconcile their suffering with a God who has bound himself in covenant to them, yet who allows his chosen people to undergo much pain.

A Midrash from *Lamentations Rabbah* takes on this task. The Midrash-maker, Rabbi Kahana, trains his imagination on a single verse from the book of Lamentations' third chapter: "This I recall to mind, therefore I have hope."

> Rabbi Kahana said: This may be likened to a king who married a lady and wrote her a large *ketubah* [marriage contract]: "so many state-apartments I am preparing for you, so many jewels I am preparing for you, and so much silver and gold I give you."
>
> The king left her and went to a distant land for many years. Her neighbors used to vex her saying, "Your husband has deserted you. Come and be married to another man." She wept and sighed, but whenever she went into her room and read her *ketubah* she would be consoled. After many years the king returned and said to her, "I am astonished that you waited for me all these years." She replied,

"My lord king, if it had not been for the generous *ketubah* you wrote me then surely my neighbors would have won me over."

So the nations of the world taunt Israel and say, "Your God has no need of you; He has deserted you and removed His Presence from you. Come to us and we shall appoint commanders and leaders of every sort for you." Israel enters the synagogues and houses of study and reads in the Torah, "I will look with favor upon you . . . and I will not spurn you" (Lev. 26:9–11) and they are consoled.

In the future the Holy One blessed be He will say to Israel, "I am astonished that you waited for me all these years." And they will reply, "If it had not been for the Torah which you gave us . . . . the nations of the world would have led us astray." . . . Therefore it is stated, "This I do recall and therefore I have hope."

Nine simple words culled from the ancient grief poem of a witness to great Jewish suffering combined with the universal image of a faithful, enduring wife— simple ingredients taken and formed into a sustaining new story. Flour, water, yeast, and sugar—and the surprising joy of watching their transformation under the pressure of intense heat.

Before "nowheresville" and before the cooking lessons, when my husband and I were discussing whether or not he should accept the job offer that would take us away from the place that had loved and nurtured us, the question solidified into certainty when he said, "Let's take our marriage out for a spin." I shared his impulse to find out how our young relationship would fare in a place where all we would have was each other. The first big test, of course, came when he handed me that infamous e-mail address.

What fascinates me now is how accurate, consoling, and ultimately freeing I found that address to be. Like any troubling verse from Torah, it expanded under my imaginative scrutiny. And like every promise from Torah, the word my husband gave me demanded my active trust in his good intentions: He was the one who had led me into exile, the one who named it for me, the one who ate and celebrated all those experimental meals I cooked up. We did indeed take our marriage out for a spin, and its endurance has depended on both of us equally.

Midrash is the richly told record of a marriage that has been tested again and again. As a result the Hebrew nation is no passive, pious wife but a hardworking partner in exile, delighting in her own resourcefulness with limited means, not afraid to experiment, nor to challenge her divine spouse, "astonishing" him with the creative use to which she puts his word.

Anyone who undertakes to learn a craft—cooking, writing, marriage, midrash—begins by following instructions and ends by abandoning them, relying instead on imagination, intuition, innovation. Likewise, every teacher of a craft hopes for the great pleasure of watching her student become a partner—a process that often requires some kind of suffering.

Suffering: The Yeast of Exile

The Catholic writer Ron Hansen expresses this paradox keenly in his novel *Mariette in Ecstasy*, through the voice of a nun who has been exiled from her monastery for over twenty years. "We try to be formed and held and kept by [God]," she writes at the end of her life, "but instead he offers us freedom. And now when I try to know his will, his kindness floods me, his great love overwhelms me, and I hear him whisper, *Surprise me.*"

TOWARD A PERSONAL PRACTICE

If you imagine your life with scripture as a marriage or another working partnership—how would you describe the dynamics of the relationship? Be honest, be humorous, be real.

6
ATTENTION
To Study Is To Play

*F*rom the moment I first began seeking to understand the "something vital" that midrash has to offer me as a writer and as a person of faith, I have been struck by the simplicity, playfulness, and almost childlike ease with which Jewish writers approach both scripture and their own creative response to its difficulties. It's hard to find a resemblance between the delight and pleasure of scripture study evident in Jewish literature, and the somber, suspicious, indignant and nit-picky picture the Christian tradition has often painted of Jewish leaders and teachers.

This is not to say the Midrashic rabbis consider their work frivolous or insignificant. Much the opposite, says the Biblical scholar Avivah Zornberg, who points to a passionate verse in Psalm 119:92: "If your Torah had not been my plaything—*sha'ashu'ai*—I should have perished in my affliction."

The play-activity of Bible study, says Zornberg, "is the secret of [Jewish] survival, enigmatic, never fully understood." She explains that the Hebrew word *sha'ashu'a* "has at its root the word *sha'a (al yish'u)*—to pay attention; in its doubled form, this becomes *sha'ashu'a*, which means play, the diffuse attention to multiple aspects of an object."

If I think about how small children go about their play, Zornberg's sophisticated definition becomes clear. My three-year-old son, Aidan, will zigzag around a single room for an hour, using just a few toys to play out three or four totally different, complex scenarios. I once met a five-year-old girl named Emma who held up the end of a telephone cord and said earnestly, "Today this is a bumble-bee, but yesterday it was a trumpet." To say a child has a short attention span is inaccurate; a child's attention, rather, is diffuse, spread out over many objects of intense focus, or using one object in many different ways.

Play—whether the game is a child's hide-and-seek or a rabbi's midrash—has a set structure, a flexible form that varies according to different time periods and cultures. Key ingredients to structured play usually include a leader, a community (real or imagined), a challenge, and an outcome (success or failure).

The folk tradition of medieval Hasidic sermons represents perhaps the high point of playfulness in the history of Midrash. Medieval European-Jewish congregations, their minds uncluttered by television, radio, or even books, took zesty pleasure in listening to a rabbi's imaginative play with scripture, expecting to be both edified and entertained as they followed the preacher's meandering path through the Bible.

The Burning Word

The structure of this midrash sermon was simple: The preaching rabbi, called the *darshan* or "midrash-maker," would always begin by reciting the assigned weekly Torah portion. Then, without commenting on that scripture at all, he would immediately recite another verse, called the "verse from afar," that seemed to bear no relation whatsoever to the original portion. The challenge for the preacher was first to raise a question or problem in this new verse, then to imaginatively show how the initial verse could be used to solve the originally stated problem, and in the process, draw from the entire exercise a spiritual lesson or insight.

In one example, a rabbi named Judah ben Simon draws his opening verse from the Torah portion Leviticus 19:23: "And when you shall come into the land, you shall plant all manner of trees." He recites this verse, then immediately cites his "verse from afar," Deuteronomy 13:5: "After the LORD your God shall you walk." These two seemingly random verses now need to be connected to a problem and a solution by the bridge of the rabbi's imaginative logic.

The problem Rabbi Simon discerns in his "verse from afar" is: How can a human being "walk after" God himself? He weaves in other verses from the Bible to intensify the question: God's path goes through "the great waters" (Ps. 77:20), God's footsteps are "unknowable" (Deut. 4:24), and God's presence is "all fire" (Dan. 7:9)—how then can any person walk as he walks?

Up to this point the rabbi takes the Bible's command literally: How can we physically walk after a divine

Attention: To Study Is To Play

being? But suddenly he turns back to the opening verse and finds a playful, non-literal way to obey the command: "But in fact the Holy One, blessed be He, from the beginning of the creation of the world, was occupied before all else with planting. For thus it is written, 'And the Lord God planted a garden at first in Eden' (Gen. 2:8), and so you shall also—when you first enter the land you should occupy yourselves first with nothing else but planting."

God plants, says the rabbi, and this is a divine activity we *can* emulate. Thus the midrash-maker arrives at the place he started, having solved the problem of the second verse and infused the first with spiritual import. "Thus it is written," he says, "'And when you shall come into the land, you shall plant all manner of trees. . . .' Why should we plant? Because planting was God's first act after the creation of the world, and in our own acts of planting, we imitate God."

TOWARD A PERSONAL PRACTICE

Letting a lectionary, or schedule of scripture, determine the passages you read can be an enormous boost to imaginative engagement with the Bible. Rather than drift toward passages that you've already established a relationship with, following a lectionary schedule will push you to surprising new places in the text. Lectionaries from many denominations can be found on the Internet or in libraries.

You can also use the unexpected events and encounters of your day as a kind of relational lectionary. Rather than regarding these as interruptions, let them inform, or even guide, your prayer and reading life.

The Burning Word

The midrash-maker's roundabout, earnestly playful journey makes sense to me, both because the connecting of literal and non-literal images is a common tool of contemporary writers, and also because my own Christian tradition, beginning with the books of the New Testament, is at its heart midrashic, seeking out and proclaiming the hidden, sometimes metaphorical connections between Biblical prophecy and Jesus' life and teachings. (Indeed, classical Midrash and the Talmud were compiled and canonized in roughly the same period as Christian Scripture).

Learning how to read the Bible with Jewish eyes has inspired both the writer and the would-be preacher in me: Perhaps the following jumbled, playful reflection on a passage from the twentieth chapter of John's Gospel could be called a Christian midrash.

As with all formal midrashim, this journey begins with a scripture text that, upon close attention, sparks a question. The following verse describes an encounter between Jesus and his disciple Mary Magdalene, three days after he has been put to death on a Roman cross:

> Jesus said to her, "Woman, why are you weeping? Whom do you seek?" Supposing him to be the gardener she said to him, "Sir, if you have carried him away, tell me where you have laid him, and I will take him away."

At first glance nothing seems problematic here. It is not surprising that Mary Magdalene is weeping, three days after her beloved teacher's death. Nor is it surprising that she would mistake him, in risen form, for the gardener, since just a few days ago she herself put his body in the tomb. But something does trouble me: Why doesn't Jesus make himself known to Mary immediately and directly? Why doesn't he call her by name? Why does he allow her to suppose, even for a moment, that he is someone other than he is?

In an indirect way, a sermon I heard a few years ago sheds some light on these questions. In this sermon, the speaker told a historical anecdote about Thomas Jefferson: that in his old age the retired president took the Christian Bible and cut out all the parts that had to do with anything supernatural, leaving in only the "wise teachings" of Jesus.

This story struck me hard as a writer, and as a lover of the Bible. What gave Jefferson the right to decide which words are sacred and true and which are not? How dare he desecrate the scriptures I held to be holy? My mind was pulsing with the question: What happened to Jesus' words, to the scraps of scripture Jefferson scissored out? Like Mary Magdalene at the entrance to a shockingly empty tomb, I wanted to know, "Where have you taken my Lord?"

To my surprise, however, instead of stewing in righteous anger, my mind started playing with, and adding to, the story. In my imagination I saw Jefferson sitting in a great wood-paneled study, musing over a large Bible and snipping away with great shears, the long strips of miracle stories and revolutionary declarations curling in the president's lap and around his ankles, or being swept imperiously into the trash can. I saw the housemaid entering the study and collecting the trash, saw her matter-of-factly adding the clutch of paper strips to the household compost heap behind the kitchen. Then I saw the heap scooped up by another servant and spread out as fertilizer in the garden.

Jefferson's marvelous garden, at Monticello: I had visited there; I knew it was one of his passions. Sitting in my hard church pew, I pictured the scraps of Jesus' rejected words being buried in that famous garden, disintegrating in its soil, being absorbed by the reaching roots of all those precious plants. I saw flowers and fruit-bearing trees pushing up through the ground, blossoming, brighter and bigger for the phenomenal word that was nourishing the soil.

Then I saw Jefferson, walking at dusk, strolling among the carefully tended rows of his garden, the various plant species and varieties marked in Latin on small tags posted in the ground. Picturing this I thought to myself, little does he know! He's reading—seeing, smelling, touching, tasting—the Bible he scorned.

I scribbled down this irrational little story in the margins of my church bulletin and tucked it away. It would be some time before I discovered the Hebrew name for what Jefferson's garden had become in my mind: a *genizah*, a burial ground for worn-out scripture. It would be some time before I discovered that Jefferson had not literally cut up pages of the Bible, but rather had copied out the "real" verses in a large ledger book. He didn't believe Jesus was God, I would learn, but he

Attention: To Study Is To Play

did believe that the teachings of Jesus, stripped of what he felt was the Bible's false religiosity, comprised, in his words, "the most sublime edifice and benevolent code of morals" ever put forth.

That they both take place in a garden is an obvious connection between the story of Jefferson's rejected scripture and Mary's post-crucifixion encounter with Jesus, but there's a deeper, more playful connection to be uncovered here. Her master's body, Mary sees, is not in the tomb. Supposing the man she does see to be the gardener, Mary pleads, "Tell me where you have laid him, and I will take him away." The literal reading of her words is straightforward. She wants to take his physical body somewhere safe, to honor it, preserve it with perfumes. Possibly she has no clear plan for what she'll do with it, but she *must know* where he has gone.

Jefferson too, I think, felt an urgent need to search out where the great teacher had been laid—though unlike Mary he believed he knew the answer. He wanted to rescue Jesus the itinerant, human philosopher. He wanted to take him and strip from his life story what he saw as the inflated claims of his Gospel biographers and the heavy shrouds of a falsely based, mystical religion.

Jefferson bent his mind to master the physical world around him. He gloried in digging his hands deep into the soil of Virginia farmland, gloried in the reports of his explorers Lewis and Clark as they pushed deep into the continent's heart. He gloried in examining the Gospel writings as things with a definable, finite history, words that were not sacred but were available as was the entire world to be scrutinized, manipulated, accepted or rejected.

Jesus too gloried in the things of this world, but rather than striving to master them he strove to join with them, so intimately that he would die for them, would become, in the words of my tradition, bread and wine, body and blood. Despite the efforts of Mary Magdalene and Thomas Jefferson, this discomfiting first-century radical Jew refuses to be rescued. Jesus has tilled *himself* into the soil, and now he cannot be "taken" by anyone. He can only be found. In what form is he found? In the form my own life takes as I seek him out, as I dig my hands into the garden of words he has left me.

Is this why Jesus does not immediately and directly make himself known to Mary? Is this why the author of the text allows her to suppose he is something other than he is? I think a medieval *darshan* would say, of course!

Underlying *every* word the Bible speaks is the intention that God be found by us. Jesus' question—"Whom do you seek?"—is not a tricky test, nor a superfluous condescension, nor yet some kind of filler stuck in by the Gospel writer. No, these words, like all the words of Scripture, are an invitation. Every uttered syllable is fertile ground for us to walk on, kneel down in, sow with the seeds of our own faithful supposing, water with the tears of our deepest searching.

Attention: To Study Is To Play

TOWARD A PERSONAL PRACTICE

Can you think of other times in the Bible when God has disguised himself? What might be the purpose of these "hide and seek" games? Is God toying with us? Or is God inviting us to gain something in the seeking that we couldn't otherwise attain?

72

In a letter to John Adams, Jefferson said of his Bible project: "I find the work obvious and easy, abstracting what is really His from the rubbish in which it is buried, easily distinguished by its lustre from the dross of His biographers, and as separate from that as the diamond from the dung hill."

This is a striking metaphor, but I must disagree with Jefferson here. Sacred Scripture is not a diamond to be culled, cut, and polished to suit our particular tastes for truth and beauty. Nor is the study of scripture simply a process of logical deduction or stringently applied historic criteria. What Jefferson calls "really His" are not simply the literal words of Jesus—but also the new life that springs up when those words get buried in the compost heap of our rubbishy lives. It is the branching new life that emerges when we allow ourselves—heart, mind, body, soul—to become a *genizah* for God's holy word.

To bring the "diffuse attention" that defines play to our scripture reading requires a broad scattering of seed upon the ground of our lives, and an openness to the surprise of what may take root and blossom there.

The Burning Word

And now I think I've found the "verse from afar" with which to close my midrash. It's from the prophet Isaiah, but I found it in a medieval *darshan's* sermon:

> It is written: "As the rain or snow drops from heaven and returns not there, but soaks the earth and makes it bring forth vegetation, yielding seed for sowing and bread for eating, so is the word that issues from My mouth: it does not come back to Me unfulfilled, but performs what I purpose, achieves what I sent it to do" (Isa. 55:10, 11). This refers to the words of Torah that God has implanted in each one of Israel; "eternal life has He planted in our midst."

This planting, this burial, this walking after God, is a continual action. In the Hebrew Bible, the prophet Hosea calls all Israel to "Take words with you and return to the LORD." The phrase implies both a continual need and a continual opportunity. I am learning that the imaginative play of making midrash can become our *teshuvah*, meaning both "return" and "response," made again and again to the God who made us.

Such planting, says one commentator, bears fruit beyond imagining, for in some mysterious way, "It is [our] annual willingness to return to God that allows the world to be sustained."

TOWARD A PERSONAL PRACTICE

Find a place and time where you can go outside and lie down and not be disturbed. Plant yourself in the ground; stretch out on the earth and try to feel its pulse. Memorize and recite Psalm 32 or read it out loud as part of your own teshuvah.

If you wish, find some way to repeat this "planting" in a city, or some other place more fraught with human tensions—try to "feel the pulse" of this new "ground." Use the same psalm, or another method, to practice teshuvah *here.*

7
IMAGINATION
Bring the Whole Tithe

*T*he year I discovered my love for language was a difficult one. I was working in Washington, D.C., as the only secretary for a small research firm, and my employer was an exacting taskmaster who timed my typing speed, staged mock phone calls (*Brring-brring!* he would suddenly say), and docked my pay for every personal call I made lasting more than two and a half minutes. I was in trouble if I missed the 7:35 bus to work, for the next one would drop me off ten minutes late, just as my boss was walking his two dogs, punctually, across the bridge and back. More than once I hid behind a corner mailbox until they passed.

The other place I hid was the office bathroom. The varnished wood door of that small room held in its grain a series of curves and whorls that I hungrily traced with my eyes. A few months later, when I'd quit the job and was flying home to Colorado in confusion (who was I? what was I doing with my life?) I looked out the airplane window and recognized with a start those same curves in the landscape below—a river was snaking its way through the flat, perfect squares of Midwest farmland.

Suddenly I understood: I needed to follow the river, pushing past the boundaries of my boss's tidy, linear, brook-no-questions, measure-up world. I didn't know where that river would lead, but I knew that traveling down its currents and turns would be my task. Soon enough I discovered the river's name was imagination, the task using words to write something that moved me, and others, to new places along its banks.

And there in the waters of language and imagination, I found midrash.

Unlike me, the rabbis who developed midrash's imaginative approach to Bible study didn't have the luxury of long reflections about how they would go about living their lives. When the Temple and its ancient, fixed worship routine was destroyed, Judaism and its people were forced to find, in the liquid, living language of Torah, a new way to meet God.

What they found first and foremost were questions—both the mundane questions of curiosity ("How come . . . ?") and the painful, profound questions of suffering ("Why this . . . ?"). Over the centuries, the answers the rabbis came up with fell into two different modes of interpretation: the *peshat* and the *derash*.

The first mode, *peshat*, looks for the literal, historically accurate, logical interpretation. The second mode, *derash*, seeks out the non-literal or "overliteral" possibilities for meaning hidden within and springing out from the text.

The Burning Word

Derash, as you might guess, is a root of the word *midrash*, and while Judaism teaches that both *peshat* and *derash* interpretations are necessary to approach full understanding of God's ever-mysterious word, it is a *derash* reading of Torah that dives into the river of imagination, while a *peshat* reading stakes itself out on the more stable intellectual shore.

A look at several different interpretations of one of the earliest verses of the Bible may help explain the distinction:

> Cain said to his brother Abel . . . and when they were in the field, Cain set upon his brother Abel and killed him.

The question raised by this text is startling and simple—*what* did Cain say to his brother? What happened in the space covered by those three little dots? The verse I've quoted here, Genesis 4:8, is from a recent Jewish translation based directly on the original Hebrew, but in most Bibles, Jewish and Christian, that disturbing gap in Cain's story does not appear. Translations as early as the Septuagint (made in 300 BCE) employed a *peshat* approach, filling in the gap by adding seven simple words: "Cain said to his brother Abel, *Let us go out to the field.*" This is a logical solution, clarifying the text without noticeably distorting it. It is a literal, historically accurate, realistic answer to a puzzling and ultimately unanswerable question.

But for the rabbis who rescued and embraced the Torah after Jerusalem's destruction in 70 CE, that gap in

Imagination: Bring the Whole Tithe

the fourth chapter of Genesis called out for something more than seven sensible words. The disturbing hole in Cain's story seemed to them not so much a Biblical oversight as a Biblical invitation, calling to their imaginations, calling for midrash: a non-literal interpretation that digs out meanings hidden within and springing out from the original text.

A collection of Midrashim called *Bereishit Rabbah* preserves some of the numerous *derash* elaborations on the sketchy quarrel between Cain and Abel that have been made through the centuries. Here is one:

> About what did they quarrel? 'Come,' said they, 'let us divide the world.' One took the land and the other the moveables. The former said, 'The land you stand on is mine,' while the latter retorted, 'What you are wearing is mine.' One said: 'Strip'; the other retorted: 'Fly [off the ground].' Out of this quarrel, "Cain rose up against his brother Abel."

Here is another:

> Said Rabbi Huna: An additional twin was born with Abel, and each claimed her. The one claimed: 'I will have her, because I am the firstborn'; while the other maintained: 'I must have her, because she was born with me.'

When faced with a problem in Scripture, *peshat* says, let's fix it, while *derash* says, let's have fun with it. Let's ride it for little bit—set the problem like a boat on the river of our imaginations and see where it takes us.

The Burning Word

These two *derash* conjectures are not based on historical evidence but rather on moral realities. They illuminate in a way the more literal *peshat* solution does not the perilous rivalry that often erupts between siblings, as well as the universal human leanings toward greed, power, and lust. The rabbis who imagined these little dialogues did what good writers do: use fiction to tell the truth. Such *derash* stories teach us, in Christian Bible scholar Eugene Peterson's words, "what the world is, and what it means to be a human being in it."

TOWARD A PERSONAL PRACTICE

Find and read Genesis 4 in a Bible. Either in conversation with a friend, or in the pages of a journal, come up with your own fictional, derash *scenarios or dialogues that reflect your own experiences of tension with siblings or peers. Does this exercise feel like a help or a hindrance to your study of this text? Are you comfortable reading it imaginatively in this way? Why or why not? Talk about this with your* hevruta, *or with yourself in a journal, or with God in prayer-conversation.*

In the Jewish view, neither of the Cain/Abel stories quoted above cancels out the other. Midrash-makers accept with reverent seriousness the task of answering the questions they claim have been deliberately left in the Biblical narrative, yet they do not insist on declaring a right answer among the many offered. Instead,

Imagination: Bring the Whole Tithe

they allow all the answers to stand side by side on the same page—like so many boats on a river, like so many streams feeding into one sea.

Midrash-makers don't simply invent circumstances that explain literal gaps in the text, announce the problem solved, and move to a new problem. Rather, they take the opportunities offered by Torah's puzzlements to ruminate and elaborate on the deeper moral issues at work in the holy words. They dip again and again into the text to bring what is hidden yet present up to the surface—and they don't ever expect the discoveries to end.

Infinite curiosity and invention are the fruits of *derash* imagination. My efficiency-oriented, *peshat*-style boss would never have understood my ongoing fascination with the patterns in the wood grain of the office bathroom door. Yet more than a decade later, I'm still searching out new ways to explain that memory and its meaning.

In the Midrash tradition, Bible stories like Cain's murder of Abel are not static, historical facts that new generations need to know merely to keep their cultural archives up to date. Nor are they simply moral tales to be used as basic training in yeshiva or Sunday school and then filed away. No, these stories are the twisting whorls in the ancient wood door of Torah, and Jewish minds have traced each spiral line a hundred times over, each time finding something new.

Three hundred years after the midrashim in *Bereishit Rabbah* were compiled, another *derash*-ic take on Cain's story was recorded, this time using wordplay and parable to illuminate the conversation between God and Cain that ensues after Abel's murder:

> The Lord said to Cain, "Where is your brother Abel?" and he said, "I don't know. Am I my brother's keeper?" (ha-shomer achi anokhi?)
>
> [Cain said:] "You God watch over all of creation and you're blaming me! This is like a thief who steals things at night and gets away with it. In the morning the watchman grabs him and says, 'Why did you steal those things?' He replied: 'I'm a thief; I haven't been remiss in doing my trade, but you're a guard; why did you fail in your duties?' Then Cain said: 'I killed him [because] you created in me the evil inclination. But You—You are the keeper (haShomer) of all things, why did you allow me to kill him? You are the one who killed him—You who are called I (Anokhi), for if you had accepted my sacrifice as you did his, I wouldn't have been jealous of him!"

Here the Midrash turns the logical interpretation of Cain's Biblical retort inside out. Instead of a plaintive attempt to avoid talking about Abel ("How should I know where he is?"), the words become a crafty accusation: "*You* are Abel's keeper, and in letting me kill him, You, God (who in other places calls himself *Anokhi*), have failed in your duty!" In the hands of the midrash-makers, the Torah's terse and economical storytelling expands into a complex picture of human recalcitrance, including Cain's smarmy, ingenious attempts to manipulate God.

Imagination: Bring the Whole Tithe

Cain is not alone, we are meant to understand, in his effort to maneuver around the inconvenience of God's truth. The imagination, like the heart, is often deceitful, often deceived.

If I didn't know this as a sibling, as a spouse, as a parent, I would know it as a writer, for I have completed no project in ten years of creative writing that did not begin as a gaping swamp, a murky marsh full of sink-holes, quagmires, half-truths, and mad claims. To tell one's truth, to tell one's world, in language, involves an astonishing amount of *mis*telling, *mis*direction and reversal. It is often hard to perceive the lies in my writing—sometimes harder still to cut them out. And this is compounded a thousand times when my subject is the Holy Bible.

Invention and imaginative discourse are necessary steps to any legitimate attempt at communicating truth and beauty with language. But what does it mean to experiment with, add to, a text that is divinely sanctioned, set apart as holy? My own religious tradition frequently pronounces the danger of manipulating the language of scripture to suit one's own misguided desires; to do so is to desecrate, even disempower, the holy revelation of God. I was taught to believe that the Bible is our bedrock, the solid ground we build our lives upon. We are much safer putting our energies into guarding that word than pulling it apart and playing around with it. Jewish tradition acknowledges that fear and that danger in the following story:

There was a Hasidic rabbi who wept every morning as he said good-bye to his wife and children before setting off to his studies. His friend asked him why. "Because," he answered, "when I begin I call out to the Lord. Then I pray 'Have mercy on us.' Who knows what the Lord's power will do to me in that moment after I have invoked it and before I beg for mercy?"

The rabbi weeps because he recognizes the real danger of conversing freely and boldly with scripture. Yet he never for one moment considers *not* entering the conversation.

The true fear of God coupled with the courage to thrust oneself imaginatively into the flame of Torah's burning bush—this is what I have found most compelling in my encounters with midrash: this astonishing balance between chutzpah and reverence, between curiosity and intimacy, between (in the words of Walter Brueggemann) vitality and fidelity.

Every morning the rabbi dares to leave the security of his home and walk to the *bet midrash,* knowing it is not his study house but God's, knowing he is called to risk his very heart, soul, mind, and body to contribute to the conversation being carried on (and on, and on) there.

Like writing, or any creative human endeavor, reading God's word is a perilous business. Too much vitality and I lose fidelity; too much fidelity and I lose vitality. To live in the balance between these opposing forces requires, I believe, a willingness to imagine, to depart from the linear and provable path. It requires a willingness to offer up everything I have: to step into the street that leads to the house where the book of YHWH lies open, to step into the river that is rushing toward the open sea.

TOWARD A PERSONAL PRACTICE

Vitality and fidelity. Chutzpah and reverence. Spend some time reflecting on the shifting balance between these diverging forces in your own life—religious, vocational, familial. Do you favor one to the detriment of the other? If you wish, write one pair of words at the top of a blank sheet of paper, with a line drawn between them down the middle of the page. Post it on a wall or tuck it somewhere handy, and use it to jot down reflections, memories, scripture verses, etc., that fall usefully into this dichotomy.

Jewish tradition holds that gaps like the one in Cain and Abel's story continually cry out *darsheni!*—interpret me! The midrash-maker's job is to answer that urgent plea with rigorous learning, with imagination, and with every action of one's daily life. Judaism considers this unfolding human response to the Bible—both *peshat* and *derash*—so crucial to the fulfillment of God's work in the world that all Jewish commentary is held to be an extension of Written Torah and is called, collectively, Oral Torah.

"Bring the whole tithe into the storehouse," says the Lord through his prophet in the book of Malachi, "that there may be food in my house." Judaism asserts that the "food" God needs from us includes our interpretations and imaginative extensions of the sacred stories that run in our blood and all through our traditions. God's storehouse, in this sense, is the Bible itself, its gaps and sudden narrative ravines making space to store the faithful supposings of those who read it.

Could it be that unless and until we bring our whole selves to reading and conversing with and living out his word, there will not be enough food in God's house? Bringing the "whole tithe" of our creative response to scripture says, "We see you, God. We will take part in your story. Amen. Yes." Perhaps telling and retelling the stories of God's reaching-out-to-us-again-and-again feeds God with the knowledge that he has reached us. *If you seek me, you will ever surely find me. I will be found by you.*

The passage from the book of Malachi concludes: "'Test me in this,' says the LORD Almighty, 'and see if I will not throw open the floodgates of heaven and pour out so much blessing that you will not have room enough for it.'" The Talmud tells of a young boy sitting in yeshiva, puzzling over this passage. How can we *test* the Lord Almighty? he says to his teacher. Doesn't Deuteronomy 6:16 say, "Do not test the LORD your God?"

The boy's rabbi explains that Hebrew has two words for "test," *nisayon* and *b'china.* The first word means testing in order to change, as when a coach tests an athlete with harder and harder exercises. The second word means testing in order to confirm what *is,* what will not change, even under testing. It is this latter test, says the rabbi, that God invites in the third chapter of Malachi.

The punctual, demanding boss I walked away from ten years ago made every workday feel like a test. Back home in Colorado I took another secretarial job, this time for a boss who *never* tested me, who chirped with delight at my every action and suggestion. This was easier, of course—but on my lunch breaks I took a spiral-bound notebook out of a drawer, hunched over my desk and dove into the river: lists of words, Bible verses, drafts of poems, wrestling romps of prayer with a God to whom I was forging a new kind of allegiance. Here was a boss who pushed me further than I'd ever been pushed, beyond the boundaries of logic, beyond the previously defined limits of my mind, heart, body, and soul. Here was a boss who asked *me* to test *him*.

The disciples in the Christian Gospel understood this joy. When Peter, riding out a storm in his boat in the middle of the night, sees Jesus come walking toward him over the swirling waves, he doesn't try to explain what's happening in logical, *peshat* terms. Instead he stands up, and calls out to his beloved Rabbi, "Lord, if it is you, bid me come to you on the water."

This is what imaginative reading ultimately requires: a willingness to step completely out of the boat and dive into the waters with a God who has declared from the beginning that we will not drown. To bring the whole tithe is to bring our whole selves, *peshat* and *derash*, to the Word who, when called to, says, "Come."

8
REPETITION
The Mirrored Voice

ood to eat, a burning flame to walk toward, seed to plant in the ground, a rushing river to enter and swim—the word of God can never be fully encompassed by one image. Its unfathomable power requires continued and renewed attempts to explain it in terms of our own experience.

I remember the first time my young son consciously recognized his own reflection in the long mirror tacked to the back of my bedroom door. He was six months old; I was holding him in my arms. He looked at me, then turned his head to the mirror—and saw me again! Surprise appeared in his eyes and he began swinging his head back and forth to try and capture this phenomenon: two mommies where there used to be one. Then a new curiosity rippled across his face as he noticed another creature in the mirror. I reached over and tweaked his nose, and I could see the senses of touch and sight collide in his brain as he felt *and* saw my fingers on what was apparently now *his* face in that mirror.

Though full of wonder at the sight, my son's reaction to the image in the glass was divided between discomfort and delight. Even at six months of age he sensed the unsettling power of self-reflection—to look in a mirror is on some level to fear what one will see.

The Christian book of James harnesses this image, and this fear, to warn us about the dangerous potential of reading the Bible: "Anyone who listens to the word but does not do what it says is like a man who looks at his face in a mirror and, after looking at himself, goes away and immediately forgets what he looks like."

James' emphasis on matching one's deeds to one's creeds is a fundamentally Jewish idea. The connection between hearing and doing, the call to mirror God's commands for right living with acts of right living in your own life—this is absolutely central to the Jewish idea of what it means to be human.

I say that I want to bring my whole self to reading the Bible—but in truth the idea of intimate conversation with scripture scares me. I myself don't *ever* do what the Bible says to any adequate extent. More often my experience can be summed up by these words from Abraham Joshua Heschel: "We have so much to say about the Bible that we are not prepared to hear what the Bible has to say about us." It's no wonder the man walks away from the looking glass of scripture, "immediately forgetting what he looks like." He can't stand the imperfect self he sees reflected in the words.

We tend to think of mirrors as neutral reflectors—infallible, and not very kind. Mirrors are polished, smooth, and hard. But the Bible does not fit this description very well. It is a passionate, insistently biased reflector. It has a rough, strangely textured surface. If it is a mirror, then looking into it will distort our reflection, as when we look into a pond or a running stream.

This distortion turns out to be a good thing: I need something to jostle me out of what James calls "forget-fulness." I need my self-perceptions to be altered—in fact I need my very self to be transformed. "When I reach the true world," said Rabbi Zusya of Anipolye, "they will not ask me why I wasn't Moses. They will ask me why I wasn't Zusya."

I caught a glimpse of that "true world" self one night some years ago when I attended a party in Washington, D.C., a miserable affair at which I felt dreadfully shy, unable to assume the casual pose of the beautiful, confident, twenty-something single gal every other woman in the room seemed to be. Around midnight I gave up the effort and went home. I crawled into bed and wormed my way under the covers. I had just enough energy to stick out a hand and grab my journal and a pen. I opened the book at random and, in darkness, scrawled the words "I am ugly." Then I fell asleep.

The next morning I woke with my hand on the open page. The curse I had written stared up at me with undiminished force, and I recognized it as utterly true. Then something strange happened: My hand reached out and picked up the pen. As if removed from my body I watched it scratch across the paper. "You are not ugly," the pen wrote, "You are Judith." And suddenly I was wide-awake. The barren wasteland of my heart had become holy ground.

This was midrash, if anything ever was—a creative interpretation of a given text. This was conversation, if anything ever was. Staring down at the words my pen had written, I found myself oddly grateful that they did not say, "You are beautiful." That would have been a lie. The words mirrored rather than erased my words; the parallel but subtly altered pronoun, verb, and adjective declared a truth that simultaneously demolished and remade my own deepest certainty.

You are Judith. Equal parts comfort and condemnation pulsed in those three small words. They were for me a transformative echo of the psalm that had run in my blood for decades: *O LORD, you have searched me and you know me. . . . Before a word is on my tongue, you know it completely, O LORD.*

If, after confronting our own failure to live up to scripture's ideals, we can manage to keep reading, can manage to drag our whole selves to the mirror even when that self seems ugly and small, we may find that being read by this holiest of texts begins to work a change in us.

TOWARD A PERSONAL PRACTICE

Transformative relationships require honesty, but even more they require presence: daily reading/conversation with the Bible will sharpen our vision and clear fog from the mirror. If you find silent, solitary reading tedious, try listening to recorded readings of scripture, or read alternating verses out loud with a partner or friend, face to face or over the phone.

In a hundred varied episodes the Bible tells the single story of a people trying and repeatedly failing to live the way their Maker has asked them to—and of that same Maker grieving their failure yet repeatedly refusing to abandon the original vision that sparked their making in the first place. The stories most of us know—Noah and the ark, Joseph and his rainbow coat, Jacob and the angel—are familiar not just because our parents and religious teachers repeated them, but also because the Bible itself repeats them.

The story of the Exodus, for example—from Israel's enslavement in Egypt to their encounter with God at Mount Sinai to their entry into the Promised Land of Canaan—is recounted fully not only in the book of Exodus, but also in the book of Numbers *and* in the book of Deuteronomy. The Christian Scriptures tell the story of Jesus' life four times. And the book of Psalms takes one hundred and fifty chapters to say a handful of things over and over: *You made us. Please save us. We're sorry. We trust you.*

When I am not turning away from the mirror of scripture out of failure to live out its precepts, I am just as likely to turn away out of boredom with its repetition. Why is all this duplication needed?

Jewish tradition teaches that the world rests on three pillars: worship, deeds, and study—and that because it leads to and inspires the first two, study is the greatest of these. Classrooms the world over have always relied on repetition as the most basic learning tool; still, I don't think the inspired writers and teachers of the Bible were using all that repetition like a hammer merely to pound truth into the dull skulls of their followers.

Rather, like the best kind of teachers, they used repetition to model their own life-giving practice of returning again and again to the mirror of scripture. This is what is meant by Judaism's emphasis on study, and it is the secret instruction hidden in James' analogy: Rather than look once into the mirror and walk away, expecting to remember and carry out perfectly what we have seen, we are to continually remind ourselves who we are by returning again and again to the mirror of scripture. *You made us. Please save us. We're sorry. We trust you.*

"He who looks into the perfect law . . . and perseveres," writes James, "being no hearer that forgets but a doer that acts, he shall be blessed in his doing." The Hebrew name for this perseverance is *teshuvah*, return and response, and the Jewish tradition has always viewed writing, reading, and speech as acts that we do, acts that matter to God. Mysteriously, the more we return and remember, the more we *become* the selves we have longed to be.

TOWARD A PERSONAL PRACTICE

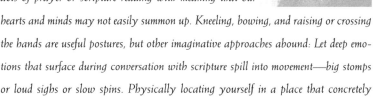

The body can be surprisingly helpful as an aid to infusing acts of prayer or scripture reading with meaning that our hearts and minds may not easily summon up. Kneeling, bowing, and raising or crossing the hands are useful postures, but other imaginative approaches abound: Let deep emotions that surface during conversation with scripture spill into movement—big stomps or loud sighs or slow spins. Physically locating yourself in a place that concretely evokes a person or event needing prayer can also energize prayer and reading.

Though I have spent much of my life meditating on and trying to live out the repeated scriptures of my faith, the Jewish practice of midrash has pushed me to look deeper into the mirror of the Bible—to find my own reflection not just in the passages that soothe or haunt me, but in every sacred word and sentence, even the most mundane.

The only verse that mentions mirrors in the Torah, for example, in the thirty-eighth chapter of Exodus, seems at first to have nothing meaningful to say to me:

> [Moses] made the laver of copper and its stand of copper, from the mirrors of the women who performed tasks at the entrance of the Tent of Meeting.

Part of a long, dry list of all the materials used to make the first Temple in Jerusalem, this verse is remarkable in only two ways—that in the original Hebrew it is set off in its own paragraph, and that in no other case is the donor of the material specifically identified. Yet over the centuries this mundane verse has been the point of origin for Midrashim exploring everything from lust to loyalty to vanity to equality to the redemption of Israel. Layer upon layer of imaginative commentary has been applied to this little verse until it glows with reflective intensity.

"Now, amongst the Israelites were certain women, dedicated to the service of God," says a Midrash from the twelfth-century sage Ibn Ezra, "who distanced themselves from worldly desire. They donated their mirrors to the Temple, as they had no further use for beautification. These women would come each day to the entrance of the Tent of Meeting to pray and to hear the details of the worship."

Eight centuries later, commentator Alex Israel examines the function and positioning of the washbasin in the Temple: Before entering the holy presence of God, priests must wash themselves in the basin placed between the tent of meeting and the altar. This commentator points out that the women who in Ibn Ezra's imagination desired to give themselves to God could never, because of their gender, actually enter the holy of holies. Instead they gathered at the entrance to the tent of meeting, where, in the refracted reflections of the mirrors they had given to build the washbasin, they could catch glimpses of the inner Temple where God dwelled.

The Burning Word

When I read these layered readings of a mundane piece of holy text I feel my soul with sudden intensity say *yes*—indirect glimpses of God are all any of us get. And with a kind of click my mind moves to yet one other mention of mirror in the Bible, written by the apostle Paul: "Now we see but a poor reflection as in a mirror, then we shall see face to face. Now I know in part; then I shall know fully, even as I am fully known."

TOWARD A PERSONAL PRACTICE

Take some time to read C. S. Lewis's great novel Till We Have Faces, *a profound midrash on Paul's mirror analogy. Stick with it—the ending is the best part.*

It's not just the text in whose dim, roughly mirrored reflection we see ourselves—it's also in the lives of those we love.

My father grew up dreaming about Brahms, Rachmaninoff, and Mozart, lying awake at night in a succession of small Texas towns listening to a scratchy radio, conducting an imaginary orchestra with a lit cigarette as his baton. In his twenties he flunked out of college and in desperation joined the army.

He had a hard time figuring out how to make his life mirror his music until he met a missionary couple where he was stationed in Germany. The cigarettes he'd used as batons had become a voice-crippling addiction, and though for weeks he resisted the couple's offer to pray for his healing, he did finally one night submit to their prayers.

Next morning the craving had disappeared, and though he didn't know it then, he would never smoke another cigarette. His missionary friends were leaving the country that same day, and as he dropped them off at the train station he said, "What do I do now?"

"Read the Bible," they said, and were gone.

The book he bought that same day now sits on my shelf. It is small, the size of his hand, and bound in thin, brown leather. After years of use the back cover has separated from the flyleaf, and specks of mildew dot the final blank pages where my father copied out verses, prayers, bits of sermons he heard over the years. I always catch my breath a little when I see those notes: They are a sacred glimpse into his early conversations with God. They are a kind of midrash.

My father, for many years now a church choir director, claims he can teach anyone to sing. He does it by a kind of mirroring. He sits down at the piano with someone who has been told all his life he is completely tone deaf. My dad instructs him to start saying a simple refrain from the Psalms, "Praise the Lord, oh my soul," quietly out loud, over and over again. Then he starts plinking on piano keys, listening keenly to the timbre of the person's speaking voice until he finds the exact note at which they are talking.

Using the piano, and using his students' own voices, my father constructs an aural mirror in which they can

The Burning Word

viscerally perceive themselves as singers. Mysteriously but unmistakably, they hear real music coming out of their mouths. "You are not tone deaf," their own music declares. "You are singing."

It is clear to me now that the students in my father's singing classes are not the only ones for whom learning music is a mirror. For them it is their first glimpse at a new self. For my father each lesson, each repeated note, is a chance to return to the mirror that first changed him. *Praise the Lord, oh my soul.* He teaches people to sing so he himself will not forget.

What I have called repetition in the Bible might most accurately be called rhythm: a carefully shaped set of recurrent stories and words that when studied closely erupts with meaning. The repetition I have in the past considered to be merely mechanical, merely tragic, or merely incantatory I now consider to be *transformative:* A work of art. A song. An ordered repetition that provides the underlying beat on which we may play out the varied notes of our own unique, improvised, musical conversation with God.

In the end we are all, in Abraham Joshua Heschel's words, "composing a song of deeds which only God fully understands." The song of our lives, brokenly yet rhythmically, mirrors the song of scripture to which we spend that life, gathered at the entrance to the altar, listening.

Repetition: The Mirrored Voice

TOWARD A PERSONAL PRACTICE

Try singing scripture as a way to enliven your approach to the text. You can fit the Bible's words to a tune you know, or just let your voice choose its own melodic path, whichever you find more helpful.

9
TRUTH
Freedom in the Rough

I was exceedingly well behaved as a teenager. I followed all the rules at school, and I never worried my parents. On weekend nights, as I was making out in my car with my boyfriend, it was not unknown for me to interrupt his kisses to look at my watch, making sure I wasn't staying out too late.

I was also exceedingly pious. At church youth group meetings, and even in gatherings with adults, I never hesitated to offer up a spoken prayer or Bible study comment, smoothly crafted, sincere, and never dull. Afterward someone always complimented me—"That was a beautiful prayer"—and I would give a little modest shrug in response.

A Midrash from the collection called *Genesis Rabbah* records that in his teenage years Abraham was pious too, though not quite so well behaved. In fact, one legend holds, he was prone to rather violent confrontations with heresy, even when the heretic was his own father:

Abraham's father was an idol-maker. He would make stone images and sell them in a shop in the market. One day, Abraham's father asked him to watch over the idols in his shop while he was away. While he was gone, Abraham seized a stick, smashed all the statues, and placed the stick in the hand of the biggest of them. When his father came back, he asked: "Who did this to the gods?" Abraham answered: "The biggest of them rose up and smashed all the others." His father replied: "Are you making fun of me? They cannot do anything! They are merely pieces of stone!" Abraham answered: "Let your ears hear what your mouth is saying!"

This story has all the best qualities of the midrashic literature I've come to love: It's cocky, crafty, and though fictional, rings true. It's anchored in scripture—the book of Joshua says Abraham's father worshiped idols, while Abraham followed the mysterious commands of one and only one God—but the rabbis who wrote it fearlessly swing out from the historical to evoke the full passion of Abraham's faith.

If I had heard and studied this Midrash in high school, my own writing might not have taken so long to break out from its straitjacket of piety. As it was, well into my college years I headed every entry in my journal with "Dear Lord," and spooled out sincere but colorless prayers for myself, my family, and what I knew of the world.

Eventually, all those nice "Dear Lords" started to make me uneasy. I wasn't praying out loud to an audience now; I was alone, and I could see those shiny prayers in print. My journal was becoming an observable record of what my tradition calls a personal relationship with my Creator—and I could see that it wasn't as close a relationship as I'd thought. I talked to God and for God and about God, but I didn't talk *with* God.

I abandoned the prayer journal and bought a new book with unlined pages. Without knowing exactly why, I began to rough up my handwriting. Sometimes I turned the book upside down to write, or closed my eyes and kept my pen moving on the page. Sometimes I set a timer for ten or twenty minutes and forced myself to record without stopping my angers, fantasies, and fears. My much-admired prayer language was left behind, for I was pushing toward something I knew I wanted but could only dimly define. Something or someone had put a stick in my hand, and I was smashing every pious statue I could find.

Rough. Blind. Upside-down. My slick prayer-pen had become a slashing ink-stick. The story of the idol shop doesn't stop at simple destruction, however, and neither did mine. Abraham's initial violence is startling, but the full impact of the story emerges when he assumes the role of teacher, of midrash-maker: Dad, he urges, pay attention to your words. Study the text coming out of your own mouth!

His true aim in swinging that stick, then, is to spark conversation. Abraham knows that language, no matter how thoughtless or rough, holds within it a life-altering creative potential.

I discovered this too, albeit slowly. At first I thought that smashing the rigid shell of all those "Dear Lords" might mean I was done with prayer entirely, but in truth my conversation with God was just beginning. In truth, God wanted, even needed, my rough new words— needed me to be thrust into a space where I could *hear* truth, and not just speak it.

On the blank page of my defiant new journal, I found my curses wouldn't stay curses—they kept turning into questions. I'd kicked out "Dear Lord" and recast the whole scene as a monologue—but I found my words stubbornly pushing toward argument, pleading, and play, forms that assume a conversational partner.

TOWARD A PERSONAL PRACTICE

Think about how your conversation with God has varied in your life. When has it felt like mostly monologue, and when has it felt like dialogue—or even full communal discourse? Are there prayer or speech practices in your life that need to be shattered and remade?

Over time, those journal pages found me pondering and reworking old texts from my pious past: scripture fragments, snatches of hymns I hadn't sung for years, analogies and stories from youth group retreats designed to illustrate basic Christian theology. Like an

The Burning Word

archaeologist, I fiddled with these archaic shards of language, turning and turning the words, trying to fit them back together into comprehensible new forms.

One story concerned a farmer who is troubled by wayward crows. Attracted by the reflection of trees in his big bay window, the birds keep hurling themselves at the glass and injuring themselves. The farmer tries in various ways to tell the crows they are being deceived and should fly to the real trees in the yard, but of course they can't understand his words. Finally he realizes that the only way to communicate with them is to become a crow himself.

God was the farmer in this story; we humans were the crows. The deceptive reflection in the window was sin, and the trees were truth, or maybe heaven. My youth group leader meant the allegory to illustrate the saving necessity of Jesus Christ, of God's needing to become human in order to save us from the false attraction of sin.

I'd heard the story, I'd gotten the point, and I thought I'd moved on. But I found the scenario following me, somehow, as I journaled and played with words, as I moved into the making of full-fledged poems and essays. I didn't want to be haunted by this simple, rather maudlin story, but there it was. Finally one day I wrote it down, and let the images run amok on the page. This poem, called "The Crow," is what emerged:

Was it because
at last
I cleaned the window

that he threw himself
against the glass?
I thought, poor crow—

he doesn't know
the evergreens
and blue sky

are behind him.
I turned back
to my page

but *whumpp*—
the bird attacked
the glass again.

His long claws
scuffled at the pane
and I yelled "Crow!

Go away!"
Again his body slapped
the glass,

again,
and then again,
and then at last

he caught my eye—
oh, prophet,
terrified.

The Burning Word

Sometimes we have to turn the story inside out; sometimes we have to rough it up to get to the truth of it. God is the crow in this poem; the speaker is the startled farmer, though instead of growing crops, she's reading and writing—farming words. That work is important, she thinks, and the crow's stupidity is an irritating distraction. But the bird persists, and finally she realizes that her book is the distraction, that the bird is not stupid but rather has something to say *to her*—something important enough to slam itself repeatedly against her windows in order to reach her.

Who is this prophet-crow? What is the message it brings? The poem ends without saying. It is a text that aims entirely at raising questions, not creating answers. It aims to make real the idea that truth, even saving truth, may be terrible, and that talking with God may require a violent shattering of what we think we know.

"You will know the truth," Jesus says in the Gospel of John, "and the truth will make you free." These words had been the bedrock of my spiritual confidence as a teenager, but now that rock was shaking beneath me. I'd thought truth was information you could know, the way you know what time it is or what street you live on: Jesus saves. I'd thought freedom was the certainty, the security you feel at knowing these things.

When I came to study midrash, however, I discovered that the Hebrew word for truth, *emeth*, is fundamentally defined as relationship—knowing truth the way you know a person. And not just static knowing, in the sense of acquaintance or identification, but the back-and-forth,

Truth: Freedom in the Rough

unpredictable, sometimes terrifying knowing that comes part and parcel with our deepest commitments.

And what kind of freedom does knowing the truth bring, then, in the Jewish sense? Not certainty, not security. Rather, the thick, rich potential in the pause between the reading of a troubled text and the beginning of your own midrash response. Rather, the wide and startling liberty of standing in a room where all the idols have been smashed.

TOWARD A PERSONAL PRACTICE

Seek out the physical experience of hearing, as a distinct thing, the silence that follows live music or text read in unison. A church, synagogue, or concert hall are helpful places to find charged silence, but you can create it yourself with gathered voices reading or singing a text.

Consider seeking out more difficult silences to sit with—in a hospital ward or court room, in a neglected neighborhood or shopping center.

Try hearing silence in your reading of the Bible, at the ends of passages you read out loud, or in wide margins you create with your own short, copied-out texts. Perhaps you will fill those spaces with your own questions and supposings. Perhaps you will leave them open, and sit quietly in the words' lingering reverberations.

There *is* bedrock in Judaism: It is Torah. Jewish bedrock is not dogma or spiritual law—it is the story of relationship with God that is told in the first five books of the Bible. Jews have always recognized the binding importance of this story, and they have also recognized that the rest of the Bible—the psalms and the prophets, the later histories, and even the Christian Gospels and epistles—are all reaction and response, all in fact midrash on the fundamental bedrock story: God created us, and God seeks to know us.

All that vast and varied conversation, all that midrash, would not be possible if the language of Torah were simple and clear. It is not. The language of these ancient stories has a texture more akin to the language of my unlined college journals: rough, blind, and upside down.

Could any story be rougher or more upside-down than the test Abraham faces as an adult, when, having become a father in his own right, he is asked to turn against his own son? The truth he so recklessly and craftily promoted as a teenager now comes back to test him:

> Then God said, "Take your son, your only son, Isaac, whom you love, and go to the region of Moriah. Sacrifice him there as a burnt offering on one of the mountains I will tell you about."

Abraham doesn't argue with God's shattering directive, nor does he plead or even question. Yet the Biblical record in the twenty-second chapter of Genesis shows that the man who even in his youth could harness the transformative power of language crafts every word he speaks with care. When Isaac asks him where they will

Truth: Freedom in the Rough

get the animal that will serve as the sacrifice, he says, "God himself will provide the lamb for the burnt offering, my son." Here again Abraham assumes the mantle of a *darshan* or midrash-maker, and his words are artfully directed at both God and the innocent boy.

God will provide the burnt offering, my son. The words put the burden of ownership of the terrible task ahead squarely on God's shoulders, and at the same time communicate total obedience; they directly answer Isaac's question with brutal honesty—*the burnt offering, my son*—while at the same time making room for God to change the outcome of the story. There is space in these utterly truthful words; there is room for a variety of interpretations—and therefore there is room for conversation.

Conversation, even with the divine, wouldn't be real unless the possibility for change existed on both sides. Abraham could choose to sheath his knife, untie the ropes around his son, and go home. God could choose to rescind his command and provide an alternate sacrifice for offering. As it turns out, the Most High does stay Abraham's hand, and points him to a ram caught in a nearby thicket. God praises Abraham's obedience, and promises him innumerable descendents that will come through Isaac and become a great nation.

All well and good. But centuries later, the Jewish conversation with this excruciating encounter isn't over: Isaac, one Midrash records, goes blind after the terror of the ordeal, and Sarah goes mute. Why? Because the imagined and specific aftermath of pain keeps the shock of the story alive. Just as the story of

Abraham and the idols breathes new life into the picture of Abraham's absolute faith in God, so the stories of lingering pain in Isaac and his family keep the full impact of relationship with the Holy One alive in the Jewish mind.

God speaks; we speak; we listen in hope for God to speak again. There is no certainty here, but when our attention to language, imagination, reverence, and courage all converge to make true conversation, true knowing, a strange kind of freedom emerges, and persists.

The stories and statutes of my own faith tradition did not portray God as an adversary, nor relationship with God as a struggle in which I might be wounded. My roughed-up journals groped toward a dim understanding of this kind of knowing, but it would take a marriage and flesh-and-blood struggle with a man more different from me than I could ever imagine to wake me up fully to *emeth*, true knowing with a God who wants to be known, but who will not be possessed.

From the very start my husband's arrival in my life shook up everything I thought I knew, and I turned to writing, and midrash, to try and make sense of it. A conversation started in the pages of my journal between my new experience of marriage and the Genesis story of blind Isaac's son, Jacob, who wrestles in the dark with a powerful stranger. Eventually, a structured poem emerged:

The night we married, making love,
my husband nudged my left hip loose

Truth: Freedom in the Rough

and I knew next day I'd be limping.
He lay beside me like a god.

"I will not let you go," I thought.
"I will not let you go until

you bless me." Funny—not until
love felled me did I fall in love,

my body opened wide, my thoughts
unhinged, my coiled mind set loose

to seize on an ancient story: God
wrestling Jacob, Jacob limping,

wounded, hip dislodged, no limping
breath in his reckless prayer: "Until

He blesses me, I'll not let this God
go!" And Jacob slept. But I, until

this long dream ends, lie stumped in thought:
he is no god who set me limping.

How does a wounded love love?
Here in the dark, love's been set loose,

been sealed. And God holds his own thoughts
till we awaken, wounded, healed.

The Burning Word

I used to be troubled by the fact that everything I write about my husband smacks of struggle, and pain, and confusion—when in truth our daily life together moves along quite joyfully. But when I think about the blessing Jacob receives from his midnight adversary, I begin to understand. The blessing is a new name, Israel, meaning "one who strives with God and lives." Holy Scripture thus warns and assures me that true relationship, true life, is not possible without intense striving: A smashing of statues. A shattering of windows. A tackling of text in the dark.

Truth: Freedom in the Rough

10
CREATION
A Fire in the Belly

Jn my late twenties, halfway through my graduate writing studies, I spent a summer in Boston, living with two younger friends who had married each other just nine months before. Though I loved being with them, it soon became clear that in many ways our lives had diverged. They were tasting all the honeymoon fruits of love; I was alone. They were putting down roots in one place; I was moving every two years to a new sublet or dorm room. They were settled in Christian beliefs and practices that had formed in childhood and college; I was questioning everything inside and around me, and writing the questions into stories, metaphors, and rhymes. When I read them my anguished, ecstatic pieces, they didn't know what to say—the language that burned in me seemed merely to bewilder them. Their groping response boiled down to one intriguing query: "Why would you need to write new poems when we already have the Psalms?"

If I'd known more at that point about the love for innovation that informs Judaism—the tradition that lies behind my friends' tradition—I might have been able to answer their question. I might have been able to say that the Psalms themselves were once new poems— deeply personal, unique constructions of language that sought to contain the passion and pain of a human people in relationship with each other and with their own Maker. As it was, I just smiled and shrugged, and made my way back to the guest room I'd furnished with a twin mattress and piles of journals and books.

Behind my friends' question, I see now, lay their reverence for the Bible. In the Jewish mind, however, reverence for God's word requires more creative attention. It requires an active, imaginative engagement with language. The psalmists who wrote those ancient prayer songs were consciously reverencing the original sacred text, Torah, by shaping its raw material into creative new forms.

TOWARD A PERSONAL PRACTICE

Find Psalm 139 in your Bible and read it out loud. Then find Deuteronomy 30:11–20 in the Torah and read it out loud. How would you describe the different form, shape, and function each text takes? Search out and contemplate the words that overlap between the two texts—can you use them to make your own reverent new form? It could be as simple as a prayer chant, or a note to a friend, or a visual collage. . . .

Questions of creativity—its usefulness, its dangers—have deeply occupied the Midrash tradition through the years. Indeed, the rabbis have not hesitated to question the creative choices of God himself. The following Midrash, found in *Genesis Rabbah,* springs from the seemingly straightforward words of Genesis 1:26, "Let us make man":

> Rabbi Simon said: When the Holy One, blessed be He, came to create the first man, the ministering angels divided into groups and parties, some saying: Let him not be created, and others saying: Let him be created . . . Mercy said: Let him be created, for he will be merciful, and Truth said: Let him not be created, for he will be all lies. Righteousness said: Let him be created, for he will do righteous deeds; Peace said: Let him not be created, for he is full of strife. . . .
>
> Rav Huna said: While the ministering angels were still arguing and disputing, the Holy One, blessed be He, created man. Then He said to them: Why do you argue? Man is already made."

Like my friends from that summer, the angels in this story are content with the way things are. They don't see the necessity for creating something new—in fact they see some worrisome dangers. Rather than rejoice at God's announcement, the angelic council takes it as a proposal to debate, and they make sound arguments. They are divine beings after all, so their insight into the future is keen: When created we humans will indeed show mercy, tell lies, and do righteous deeds.

We will also, says the angel called Peace, be "full of strife." Peace is the one angel who may have a hint that God is not going to be swayed by the debate, for even while casting a "no" vote, Peace speaks in the present tense: Let him not be created, for he *is* full of strife.

Why should we make something new when what we already have is so good? The Midrash doesn't answer the implicit question. Instead, without justifying himself, the Holy One goes ahead and makes this new thing, the human being.

We are created with marvelous powers; we can choose or refuse to practice mercy, truth, and justice. But true to the angel's prediction, God hasn't given us a choice about strife—most all of our lives are full of it.

We were made with what the writer Sam Keen calls a "fire in the belly." It's the fire that sparked the marriage of my friends, who have now moved past the honeymoon stage and are engaged in the creative strife of raising two children. It's the fire that sparked my ongoing fascination with language and midrash. And it's the fire that sparks the following tale, both in the cruelty of a man who tells lies about his rabbi and in the passion of that rabbi's innovative response:

> A man who had falsely slandered the rabbi in his town had a change of heart, and went to the holy man to seek his pardon. "What must I do to repair my sin?" he asked. The rabbi instructed the man to

get a pillow, rip it open and spread its feathers on the wind, and then return to him. The man quickly did as he was told. Upon his return, the rabbi said, "There is one task remaining: go find and collect all the feathers, and bring them to me." The man gasped, "That's impossible!" And the rabbi replied, "Yes. It is as impossible for you to re-gather those feathers as it is for you to repair the harm that your slander has worked on me and my town."

Like the other questions in this chapter, and in this book, no clear answer is given to the slanderer's query, "What must I do to repair my sin?" The rabbi refuses to give him forgiveness, but he does give him—and those who read the tale—something quite valuable: a fresh, tangible experience of the power of lies that will likely never be forgotten. With symbolic action and with words the rabbi creates a new container for the fire that burns in the heart of a liar, that burns in the belly of one about whom the lies are told.

The writings of my own Christian tradition certainly offer this kind of vivid parable, but they have also tended to offer language that functions less like creative crucibles of felt experience and more like glass jars with intellectual labels: Annunciation. Incarnation. Atonement. Epiphany. Hermeneutics. Omniscience. Theodicy.

These words are durable, compact, and useful for summing up long histories of debate on the deepest theological questions. But you will not find many of them in the Talmud or Midrash collections—and you will find none of them in the Torah. For Jews, words cannot function as labels that point to a separate spiritual reality. The words themselves must hold and convey that reality. Jewish words come from the fire of the belly, not the cool logic of the head.

In the solitude of my friends' guest room that summer in Boston, I tried to write from my belly. Though I didn't yet know the vocabulary or history of the tradition behind my tradition, I see now that I was engaged in a kind of pre-Midrash. I wrote a poem called "Annunciation" that never defines the word, that never mentions Mary or the angel who announces the miracle of her virgin pregnancy. Instead it tries to contain, in contemporary images and rhythms, something of the enormous surprise of that encounter, to evoke something akin to the gasp—*that's impossible!*—of the man in the rabbi's tale:

118

> Into the rushing dark
> a hundred starlings rise,
> a hundred breaths, two hundred,
> oh! a thousand climb the air,
> their single body swelling like a lung
> inhaling sky and still
> more sky, wings lifted into light
> already fallen as they turn
> and dive to girder nests beneath the highway.

I'm hushed in my fast car, just
passing the bridge when they're
up again, wavering now in the dusk
like a casual hand, raised for a moment
then dropped—I am
reeling,
swept to the edge of the highway and left

with what but to follow,
wholly, smitten,
this summons so swiftly, so
distantly given.

TOWARD A PERSONAL PRACTICE

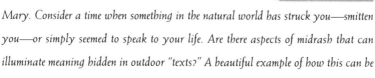

The poem above is as much a conversation with nature as
with the scriptural event of the angel's announcement to
Mary. Consider a time when something in the natural world has struck you—smitten
you—or simply seemed to speak to your life. Are there aspects of midrash that can
illuminate meaning hidden in outdoor "texts?" A beautiful example of how this can be
done is Annie Dillard's short book Teaching A Stone To Talk.

It took me three months to write "Annunciation."
Every day I would dress up in nice clothes and walk
from my friends' house to the subway station, carrying
in a shoulder bag my sack lunch and a sheaf of words—
a cloud of starlings, a visiting angel with a powerful
raised hand. From the subway station I'd catch various

trains to various offices where secretaries were taking time off for summer vacations. All day long, all I had to do was answer the phone and pass it on to someone else. I sat at the desk I was assigned and spent hours arranging and rearranging words about birds on the page.

I have said that the process of making midrash requires four simple steps: choose a text, find a problem or question, draw an answer out of your imagination, and find someone to argue it or expand it. I didn't know I was making midrash that summer, and I didn't follow the steps in any kind of linear order—but I see now that all those hours of fiddling with language were powered by an ancient fire in my belly, a fierce need to create that trumped all the reasons why I shouldn't.

A question, not a text, sparked that fire. *Why make new poems when we already have the Psalms?* My friends' innocent words had high-stakes implications for me; I could have rephrased their question into any number of fearful versions. Why have I borrowed money I don't have to pay for mastering a skill no one will ever pay me to use? Why am I putting my passion into little rhyming scribbles when my friends are putting their passion into each other, every night? Why call myself a Christian when I see in the Bible and in the world more questions than answers, more uncertainty than certainty?

These were crucial life concerns. So why, instead of giving time to them, did I turn the attention of my imagination solely and obsessively upon my memory of a massive swell of starlings I had seen on my highway drive up to Boston?

I didn't know. I didn't care. For those three months, the most important work of my life was to translate the single movement of a thousand birds and the wonder of my seeing them into plain black letters on white paper.

When I finished the poem, I felt huge. And tiny—powerful and powerless at the same time. I had done it! I'd made a container of words for those uncontainable birds. But those words turned out to be more than a simple nature poem—they turned out to be a summons. A call, simply put, to say yes to my life, to the as-yet-unrevealed life that God was giving me. That call was the answer to the fearful questions I'd been dogged by, though it made as little sense to me as to those debating angels who question God's decision to create—as little sense as God's answer to Mary when she says, how can I bear a child when I have not been with a man?

In truth, the idea of using the title of my poem to compare that astonishing winged cloud with the angel Gabriel's announcement to a virgin girl didn't occur to me until after the body of the poem had been written. Even then, the full meaning of the connection remained hidden from me; all I knew was that working it out had helped me through that lonely summer.

When I read Mary's story now in the first chapter of the Gospel of Luke, I see that after the angel leaves, Mary makes midrash. Out of the blue she's been simultaneously blessed and stricken by a divine hand, and she feels tiny. Huge. She's got to put her feelings into words or she'll explode—and so she sings a song: *My soul doth magnify the Lord. . . . For he that is mighty hath done to me great things; and holy is his name. And his mercy is on them that fear him from generation to generation.*

Like all midrash, her words spring out of scripture— her song is full of lines taken from the Psalms, a text with which she would have been intimately acquainted. But the song is also uniquely hers, a made thing, a new creation fired by the urgent need to make sense of her own strange world and time.

Mary's soul, she says, "magnifies" God—that is to say, her own words amplify, enlarge, and clarify God's. This is a marvelous way to describe the Jewish way of reading the Bible. She says also that God's mercy is earned by those that "fear him from generation to generation." Here Mary claims for herself the need and right to reverence God with new forms—trusting God to be merciful when those forms are broken or insufficient. Generations later, her song in scripture also claims that need and right for me.

The study tradition of midrash makes explicit an idea that Mary's impulsive song bears out: through our own creative reading and making, God can speak to us. At any given time, what will the Holy One say? It is impossible for us to know. As impossible as to follow a flock of birds on foot; as to gather back a liar's words; as to bear in your belly's fire the very person and power of God.

TOWARD A PERSONAL PRACTICE

A simple way to experiment with making midrash is to copy out a text on paper, leaving double or triple spaces between each line. Try this with Mary's song in Luke 1, or with an older text she echoes, Psalm 34. Then fill in the spaces with your own dialogue, images, memories—or, alternatively, a newspaper report, political speech, or list of statistics. How does this pastiche of old and new words, this new creation, "magnify" God's word?

|

11
REVELATION
Word Without End

From the start, my encounters with Jewish Midrash have made me feel like a child. Swinging my head back and forth in amazement like a baby facing a mirror with his mommy, I see myself in one tradition, and in another tradition I see myself as well. The curiosity, excitement, and trepidation that first widened my eyes have not abated after all this learning, and I am grateful, for as it turns out, the often uncomfortable double vision of reading Midrash as a Christian has given my conversations with the Bible new clarity and focus.

My reading of Jesus, in particular, has grown sharper and brighter under a midrashic gaze. His followers called him Rabbi, and my reading of the Gospel stories show him to be that and more. The story of his encounter with two disciples late in the Gospel of Luke, for example, shows a playfully hidden God who seeks out intimate conversation with his followers. He waits until the pair act on their curiosity and urge him to stay, and when he finally reveals himself, his words set them on fire.

The story begins with what seems like its end: Two disciples of Jesus are walking and talking on the road to a town called Emmaus, three days after their teacher has been put to death. For this pair of first-century Jews, the story they thought they were living is over: Jesus was not, after all, the One whom the Scriptures prophesied would come to save Israel and the world. Rome has crucified this would-be Messiah, the dream is at an end, and now they are walking away from Jerusalem, back to where they came from, talking together and trying to sort through where things went wrong.

Before they reach Emmaus, however, a stranger joins the conversation and, like a true *darshan*, a midrash-maker, he turns the story's ending on its head:

> While they were talking and discussing, Jesus himself came near and went with them, but their eyes were kept from recognizing him.
>
> And he said to them, "What are you discussing with each other while you walk along?" They stood still, looking sad. Then one of them, whose name was Cleopas, answered him, "Are you the only stranger in Jerusalem who does not know the things that have taken place there in these days?" He asked them, "What things?" They replied, "The things about Jesus of Nazareth, who was a prophet mighty in deed and word before God and all the people, and how our chief priests and leaders handed him over to be condemned to death and crucified him. But we

had hoped that he was the one to redeem Israel. Yes, and besides all this, it is now the third day since these things took place. . . .

Then he said to them, "Oh, how foolish you are, and how slow of heart to believe all that the prophets have declared! Was it not necessary that the Messiah should suffer these things and then enter into his glory?" Then beginning with Moses and all the prophets, he interpreted to them the things about himself in all the scriptures.

As they came near the village to which they were going, he walked ahead as if he were going on. But they urged him strongly, saying, "Stay with us, because it is almost evening and the day is now nearly over." So he went in to stay with them. When he was at table with them, he took bread, blessed and broke it, and gave it to them.

Then their eyes were opened, and they recognized him; and he vanished from their sight. They said to each other, "Were not our hearts burning within us while he was talking to us on the road, while he was opening the scriptures to us?"

As a Christian I have heard this resurrection story many times, but when I try to read it with Jewish eyes, I get a surprise: I had assumed that it was Jesus' sudden physical manifestation that set his followers' hearts on fire—but when, exactly, were their hearts burning? *On the road, while he was opening the scriptures.* While he was just a stranger to them, while all he was giving them was words, their inmost beings kindled and caught fire.

The tradition I grew up in celebrates the *information* in this story: Jesus is alive, and he fulfills the ancient descriptions of Messiah, the Savior of the world. But in the tradition behind my tradition—Judaism—revelation cannot be reduced to facts alone; midrash celebrates *conversation* more than information. The fire of divine revelation requires kindling, and the kindling in this story, as in the practice of midrash, is the troubled human exchange that draws the curiosity of a hidden God.

"What are these words that you're exchanging with one another as you are walking?" the stranger says, and when Cleopas says, "Don't you know?" He says, "No, tell me." The hidden Jesus wants the disciples to give him their words so that he can give them back—connect their tragic, present-moment pain to ancient Biblical promises, and with holy midrash set them ablaze.

Oh how foolish you are! Jesus says to the pair, giving the conversation a playfully argumentative twist. The *darshan* is scolding them now—surely you could have figured this out for yourselves—but he is doing something deeper as well. He is breaking their words, that they might be put back together as revelation.

He does the same thing, in this story, with bread. "Stay with us," the two men urge the stranger, and when he is seated at their table he takes the gift of their bread and blesses it, and breaks it, and gives it back to them to eat. "Then their eyes were opened, and they recognized him." The hidden God is thus revealed in the intimate tearing open of two seekers' freely offered food, freely offered words.

TOWARD A PERSONAL PRACTICE

One place we are sure to find the gift of words freely offered is in church or synagogue every weekend. The pastors and rabbis who stand and speak before their congregations would like nothing better than to have their words generate new discussion, even argument—to have their words break in the mouths and minds of their hearers. Consider reciprocating the gift of a sermon with the gift of a conversation.

You may also wish to look for other "freely offered words" to "break" and "give back" through conversation: on the Internet, at a town hall meeting, in the op-ed pages of your newspaper.

Breaking is a necessary step in any creative endeavor— a painful but ultimately rewarding application of the ancient Jewish dictum: *Turn it and turn it again, for everything is contained therein.* The "J-word poem" I wrote for my Wednesday night workshop, for example, was broken and remade several times before it reached wholeness. What I thought was the final version ended like this:

> Jesus with eyes of wild oak and sung honey
> Jesus with eyes full of desert

Eyes full of mirror and a roaring horizon
Eyes of a bird beyond reach of the gun

My fellow writers loved it, and at first I felt I'd succeeded in breathing new life into a holy name. But three years later a magazine editor pointed out the theological error in my poem's ending. Jesus might be compared to a "bird beyond the gun"—but he wasn't, as I'd written, beyond *reach* of the gun. To say so was to negate both the sacrificial death and the saving power of that death that lie at the very heart of the Christian tradition.

Oh how foolish you are, and how slow of heart to believe! God's saving language is not about avoiding "the gun," avoiding the pain of full engagement with life; God's saving language is about enduring through it and transforming it. I spent hours as a child gazing at my picture of Jesus on the wall, but until I struggled, and struggled again, to put that gaze into words, I didn't know that eyes—even Messiah eyes—don't fill with honey and song and horizon without suffering, without the imaginative vision that is born only in suffering's heat.

Jewish midrash-makers know that heat, and pass through it by way of reverent, daring conversation with Torah. In the years since I broke and remade that poem I too have known suffering, and have found saving refuge in wrestling with scripture. But the clearest picture I have of the Emmaus disciples' burning exchange with the Bible comes not from a *bet midrash* or writing workshop but from a tent in a refugee camp in Chiapas, Mexico.

The Burning Word

The camp had been established by the Mexican government for a group of Guatemalan farmers exiled by a violent civil war, and I visited there with a friend's relief organization during the summer's-long gap that opened up when I quit the secretarial job that had worn me down in Washington, D.C.

I spent two nights in the home of a woman I remember only as Felicita. She wasn't there when my friend and I arrived, but when the tiny, smiling woman pushed into the tent around dinnertime, the humble surroundings suddenly glowed. She'd had some good news, she told us: Her Bible study had asked her to start a new group and be its leader—something a woman had never been allowed to do. Over a meal of corn soup and black beans she dazzled us with her account of the Scriptures and the way they were opening her eyes to her place in the story of God's world.

That story, I learned later, was full of suffering: Every person in the makeshift camp had seen family members murdered or simply taken away. But the words that flowed out of our diminutive *darshan* that night, scripture and interpetation running together in a wondrous rush, were as full of imaginative power as any sermon or midrash I've encountered.

The day before I met Felicita, I spent ten hours traveling twelve miles from a hostel in San Cristobal to the refugee camp set up by a river.

My friend and I made our way to the dusty town of Comalapa, waited an hour, then climbed onto the back of the pickup truck that finally arrived. Brooke said hurry, get a seat or we'll have to stand the whole way. Around the bodies of his fifteen passengers the driver packed crates of bananas, bags of rice and black beans, boxes of soap, more crates of avocados and tomatoes, and our two big American backpacks. At the last minute he tried to cram in a crate with two brawling pigs, but the human cargo resisted with a moan and several nasty looks.

We took off in a swirl of dust, a few more men running and jumping onto the back of the truck, graceful in their pointy boots, baggy jeans, and bared muscles. I perched precariously on a narrow board with my arm wrapped around a little girl—partly to keep her from flying out, partly to keep my own balance, and partly to feel her childish body close to mine.

Looking out the back of the open truck I saw nothing but dirt road curving into thick tropical forest; looking out the front I saw again only the curving road and the dark curtain of trees. Suddenly, my entire world was reduced to this ongoing road, this lumbering truck, this child's weight against my hip. Any place we might have come from and any place we might have been going had long ago been swallowed up by time and those trees. There was only the road—and though we were clearly moving, we were just as clearly never going to arrive.

I am the Way, the Truth, and the Life. The Gospel words throbbed in my blood to the beat of the old truck's tires. More words took up the rhythm: *Were not our hearts burning within us while he was talking to us on the road?* And

The Burning Word

suddenly I saw it, again and for the very first time: God here. God now. God swaying on the bench beside us, Bibles open on our laps, always on the road to a lush and dusty nowheresville. The ancient, ever-new practice called midrash has put me back on that road.

Acknowledgments

This book would not exist without the help and encouragement of many people. I am especially grateful to my editor, Lil Copan, who told me from the start that the more I admit I do not know the answers, the better my writing will be. She has championed me and pushed me beyond where I thought I could go. Thanks also to my teachers Scott Cairns, Suzanne Gardinier, Marie Howe, Rabbi Benay Lappe and The Curriculum Institute, and to my precious, committed circle of readers: Kevin Kunst, Lavetta McCune, Gayle Boss, Amy Enright, Sara Belk, Judy Oulund, Jean Linzee, and Karen Singer. Special thanks to the Unicycle collaborative: Stu Hancock, Joy & Scott Sawyer, Caroline Jarboe, Gina Bria, Jim Vescovi, Katie Towler, Jim Sparrell, Sheryl Cornett, and Joey Earl Horstman. By word and by example you have dared me to stay up on the spinning wheel. Finally, without the love and support of The Stony Brook School community I could not have completed this project. From headmaster to students to faculty and staff, you are a people of true "vitality and fidelity."

Invaluable research assistance came from the Emma S. Clark Public Library in Stony Brook, NY, and the

Bull Street and Armstrong-Atlantic State University libraries in Savannah, GA, and also from Rabbi Alan Londy, who encouraged me early on and led me to the work of Avivah Zornberg. Thanks to Ron Minor and Cassandra Visconti for assistance in preparing the manuscript, to Melinda Johnson, Crystal Kim, and Ann Janowski for hours of free babysitting, and to Ben and Susi Leeming for their hospitality at the start and finish

of it all. The buoyant, sacrificial support of my husband and son renders me, as always, speechless.

Three books have been essential companions in my own writing and deserve mention here: *God In Search of Man*, by Abraham Joshua Heschel; *Back To The Sources: Reading the Classic Jewish Texts*, by Barry W. Holtz and others; and *The Bible Makes Sense*, by Walter Brueggemann. If reading my book leads you to read these, my own small effort will have been a success.

Notes

1
INTIMACY: *Turn & Return*

p. 1. *"You are reading the Hebrew Bible—but are you reading it with Hebrew eyes?"* personal conversation with Scott Cairns, The Glen Workshops, Colorado Springs, CO, 1998.

p. 2. *"Turn your eyes upon Jesus . . . His glory and grace."* Lyrics by Helen H. Lemmel. (Grand Rapids, MI: Singspiration, Inc., 1950), Used by permission.

p. 4. *"The Talmud says God himself studies the Torah every day."* Robert Goldenberg, "Talmud," in Barry Holtz, ed., *Back to the Sources: Reading the Classic Jewish Texts* (New York: Touchstone, 1984), 167.

p. 4. *"Turn it, and turn it again," the Talmud says, "for everything is contained therein."* Rabbi Ben Bag Bag, Talmud, Pirkei Avot.

p. 7. *"If you seek me . . . found by you."* Jeremiah 29:13, 14, author's paraphrase.

p. 7. *"In the beginning was the Word . . . among us."* John 1:1, 14a. RSV.

p. 7. *. . . written roughly around the same time that the ancient rabbis began reinterpreting the Torah . . .* See article on Mishnah and Tannaim at (see next page) http://www.encyclopedia.com/html/T/Tannaim.asp and article on Gospel of John at http://www.newadvent.org/cathen/08438a.htm

p. 9. *"Now to him . . . be glory."* Ephesians 3:20-21a.

pp. 10-11. *"There was a king of flesh and blood . . . to spin a garment from it."* Talmud, Seder Eliyahu Zuta, Chapter 2, as found in Barry Holtz, ed., *Back to the Sources: Reading the Classic Jewish Texts* (New York: Touchstone, 1984), 28. Used by permission. This story strikingly parallels Jesus' parable of the talents, found in Matthew 25:14–30.

p. 12. *. . . in rabbinic Judaism . . . Bible study replaced Temple worship* Rabbi Benay Lappe, lectures on Talmud and Midrash. The Curriculum Initiative Summer Institute, Princeton University, June 2001.

2
REVERENCE: *The Word Is Real*

p. 16. *It's why Orthodox Jewish women still . . . kiss the Torah scroll* Mary Blye Howe, *A Baptist Among the Jews.* (Hoboken, NJ: June 2001), 9.

p. 16. *It's why the first act of young boys . . . in medieval yeshivas was to lick smeared honey.* Jonathan Rosen, *The Talmud and the Internet: A Journey Between Worlds* (New York: Picador USA, 2001), 25.

p. 16. *It's why the Torah . . . is buried in a* genizah
More information about this practice can be found at www.jewishencyclopedia.com.

p. 18. *Holy words are things to be savored.* For a more in-depth discussion of the distinction between Greek (Christian) and Hebraic views of language, see Scott Cairns, "Sacred Tradition and the Individual Talent" in *Image: A Journal of Religion and the Arts,* Winter, 1999-2000, No. 25, 73–82.

p. 18. *"When your words came, I ate them."* Jeremiah 15:16a.

p. 18. *"Eat this scroll. . . ."* Ezekiel 3:3.

p. 18. *"Listen to me, and eat what is good. . . ."* Isaiah 55:2b.

p. 18. *"The scriptures teach us how to read the scriptures."* D. Harman Akenson, *Surpassing Wonder: The Invention of the Bible & the Talmuds* (Chicago: The University of Chicago Press, 1998), 7.

p. 20. *"language is 'rich and malleable . . . the very . . . sounds of it.'"* Mary Oliver, *A Poetry Handbook* (New York: Harcourt Brace & Co., 1994), 34.

p. 22. *"The word of God is not an object of contemplation . . . more powerful than all thunders."* Abraham Joshua Heschel, *God in Search of Man: A Philosophy of Judaism* (New York: Farrar, Straus & Giroux, 1955), 197.

p. 23. *". . . indeterminate enormity . . ."* This phrase and idea appears in a number of articles and poems by Scott Cairns.

p. 24. *Elohim . . . El Shaddai . . . El-Olam . . .* More information about God's names can be found at http://www.jewishvirtu-allibrary.org/jsource/Judaism/name.html#Names.

p. 25. *"Now what I am commanding you . . ."* Deuteronomy 30:11, 14; 11:18.

3
CURIOSITY: *The Word Is Burning*

p. 27. . . . . *God dictated to Moses the entire Torah . . . down through the ages."* Read more about this in Jacob Neusner, *The Oral Torah: The Sacred Books of Judaism* (San Francisco: Harper & Row Publishers, 1986).

p. 28. *"Now Moses, tending the flock . . . he was afraid to look at God."* Exodus 3:1–6. NJPS.

p. 29. *"Perhaps that is the meaning of the burning bush . . . He must hide His power."* Abraham Joshua Heschel, *God in Search of Man: A Philosophy of Judaism* (New York: Farrar, Straus & Giroux, 1955), 191.

p. 34. *As Israel's ancient priests knew . . . before entering . . . the Holy of Holies* Katherine Towler, "A Writer's Life: Showing Up is Half the Work," in *Mars Hill Review*, Number 17, 9.

p. 34. *Torah existed before . . . the world . . . white fire engraved with black fire.* This well-known Jewish image is described in Rabbi Avi Weiss, "Shabbat Forshpeis: A Taste of Torah in Honor of Shabbat" at

http://www.hir.org/a_weekly_gallery/9.28.02-weekly.html.

pp. 36-37. *One legend says that when the great prophet dies . . . where God is still working.* This story is summarized from the Babylonian Talmud, Menachat, 29b.

p. 37. *During the ritual* seder *meal, each child . . . is obliged to ask four traditional questions. . . .* Found in the Arba'ah Banim section of the Passover Haggadah.

4
COMMUNITY: *To Argue Is To Love*

p. 39. *"Make for yourself a teacher. Acquire for yourself a friend . . . benefit of the doubt."* This saying is from the Pirke Avot in the Talmud.

pp. 39-40. *As young children in* yeshiva *. . . of a text . . . God commands them to interpret.* Rabbi Benay Lappe, Lectures on Talmud and Midrash. The Curriculum Initiative Summer Institute, Princeton University, June 2001.

pp. 40-41. *The Rabbinic Bible . . . across ages and continents.* Jordan S. Penkower, "The Development of the Masoretic Bible," in *The Jewish Study Bible* (New York: Oxford University Press, 2004), 2082.

p. 41. *The Rabbinic Bible has been called society's first 'hypertext.'* Jonathan Rosen, *The Talmud and the Internet: A Journey Between Worlds* (New York: Picador USA, 2001), throughout.

p. 41. *"They lie there next to each other on the page. . . ."* Daniel Stern, "Midrash and Jewish Interpretation" in *The Jewish Study Bible* (New York: Oxford University Press, 2004), 1874.

pp. 44-45 *". . . And Resh Lakish died. . . . Where are you?"* This Midrash from the Talmud, Ketubot 103b is found in *On The Nature of Being Human: An Ethics Sourcebook*, published by The Curriculum Institute, www.thecurriculum.org, 184. Used by permission.

pp. 46-47. *"It has been taught: On that day Rabbi Eliezar . . . he replied, saying, 'My sons have defeated me, My sons have defeated me!'"* This Midrash from the Talmud, Baba Metzia, 59b is found

http://www.come-and-hear.com/babamezia/babamezia_
59.html#Partb.

pp. 47-48. *Ultimately, from a mainstream Jewish perspective, it is more
important to be in conversation with each other and get it "wrong"* . . .
comes through and from a limited, flawed human being. These statements are based on personal conversation with Rabbi
Benay Lappe, master teacher of Svara Yeshiva, 2005.

p. 48. *"foolish controversies and genealogies* . . . *are unprofitable and
useless."* Titus 3:9.

p. 48. *".* . . *will not quarrel.* . . . *voice in the streets."* Matthew 12:19.

5
SUFFERING: *The Yeast of Exile*

p. 54. *"Each line begins with a succeeding letter of the Hebrew alphabet.*
Daniel Grossberg, "Lamentations: Introduction" in *The
Jewish Study Bible* (New York: Oxford University Press,
2004), 1588.

p. 55. *"I am the man* . . . *darkness without any light."* Lamentations
3:1,2. RSV.

p. 55. *".* . . *the steadfast love of the Lord never ceases.* . . . *"*
Lamentations 3:22. RSV.

p. 55. *"The* LORD *is my portion* . . . *hope in him."* Lamentations
3:24. RSV.

pp. 59-60. *"Rabbi Kahana said* . . . *this I do recall and therefore I
have hope."* This Midrash from Lamentations Rabbah is
taken from Barry W. Holtz, "Midrash" in Barry W. Holtz,
ed., *Back to the Sources: Reading the Classic Jewish Texts.* (New
York: Touchstone, 1984), 183-84. Used by permission.

p. 62. *"We try to be formed . . . and I hear him whisper,* Surprise me." Ron Hansen, *Mariette In Ecstacy* (New York: HarperPerennial, 1991), 179.

6
ATTENTION: *To Study Is To Play*

p. 64. *". . . the Hebrew word* sha'ashu'a *'has at its root the word* sha'a (al yish'u)—*to pay attention . . . becomes* sha'ashu'a, *which means play.'"* Avivah Gottlieb Zornberg, *The Particulars of Rapture* (New York: Image/Doubleday, 2001) 114-115.

p. 65. *"The preaching rabbi, called the* darshan *. . . 'verse from afar.'"* For more information on this topic see David Stern, "Midrash and Midrashic Interpretation" in *The Jewish Study Bible* (New York: Oxford University Press, 2004), 1872-73.

pp. 64-65. *In one example, a rabbi named Judah ben Simon draws his opening verse . . .* This Midrash from Leviticus Rabbah, along with its explanation, is found in Barry W. Holtz, "Midrash," in Barry W. Holtz, ed., *Back to the Sources: Reading the Classic Jewish Texts* (New York: Touchstone, 1984), 199-200. Used by permission.

p. 67. *"Jesus said to her, 'Woman, why are you weeping?'. . .' and I will take him.'"* John 20:15. RSV.

p. 70. *"the most sublime edifice and benevolent code of morals"* This and all other quotations from Jefferson's correspondence are taken from Edwin S. Gaustad, *Sworn on the Altar of God: A Religious Biography of Thomas Jefferson* (Grand Rapids, MI: Wm. B. Eerdmans Publishing Co., 1996), 115.

p. 72. *"I find the work obvious and easy . . . diamond from the dung hill."* Gaustad, 119.

Notes

p. 72. *"It is written: 'As the rain or snow drops . . .* "*eternal life has He planted in our midst.*"'" This commentary from the Hasidic text Sefat Emet is found in Arthur Green, "Teachings of the Hasidic Masters," in Barry W. Holtz, ed., *Back to the Sources: Reading the Classic Jewish Texts* (New York: Touchstone, 1984), 398. Used by permission.

p. 73. *"Take words . . . to the* LORD." Hosea 14:2.

p. 73. *"It is [our] annual willingness . . . to be sustained."* Green, 397.

7

IMAGINATION: *Bring the Whole Tithe*

p. 76. *Over the centuries . . . the* peshat *and the* derash . . .
For a much more detailed discussion of these terms see Edward L. Greenstein, "Medieval Bible Commentaries" in Barry W. Holtz, ed., *Back to the Sources: Reading the Classic Jewish Texts.* (New York: Touchstone, 1984), 215–257.

p. 77. *"Cain said to his brother . . . and killed him."* Genesis 4:8. JSB.

p. 78. *"About what did they quarrel? . . . because she was born with me."* These two Midrashim from Bereishit Rabbah are taken from Rabbi Ischa Waldman, "Filling in the Gaps." http://www.myjewishlearning.com/texts/Midrash/MidrashAggadah/FillingGaps.htm. Used by permission.

p. 79. *"what the world is . . . to be a human being in it."* Eugene Peterson, *Leap Over A Wall* (New York: HarperSanFrancisco, 1997), 4.

p. 81. *"The Lord said to Cain, 'Where is your brother Abel?' . . . 'I wouldn't have been jealous of him!'"* This Midrash from Midrash Tanhuma is taken from Barry W. Holtz, "Midrash," in Barry W. Holtz, ed., *Back to the Sources: Reading the Classic Jewish Texts* (New York: Touchstone, 1984), 195. Used by permission.

p. 83. *"There was a Hasidic rabbi . . . before I beg for mercy."* This story is found in Annie Dillard, *The Writing Life,* (New York: HarperPerennial, 1989), 8-9.

p. 83. *". . . vitality and fidelity."* Walter Brueggemann, *The Bible Makes Sense* (Cincinnati, OH: St. Anthony Messenger Press, 2003), 119.

p. 84. *"Jewish tradition holds . . . cry out 'darsheni!'—interpret me!"* Waldman, http://www.myjewishlearning.com/texts/Midrash/Midrash Aggadah/FillingGaps.htm.

p. 84. *"Bring the whole tithe into the storehouse. . . ."* Malachi 3:10.

pp. 85-86. *"Test me in this . . . it is the latter test, says the rabbi, that God invites. . . ."* Jacob Solomon, "Parashat Metzora/Shabbat Hagadol 5763" in *Between the Fish and the Soup* at http://www.shemayisrael.co.il/parsha/solomon/archives/metzora63.htm.

8
REPETITION: *The Mirrored Voice*

p. 88. *"Anyone who listens to the word . . . forgets what he looks like."* James 1:23-24.

p. 88. *"We have so much to say about the Bible that we are not prepared to hear what the Bible has to say about us."* Abraham Joshua Heschel, *I Asked for Wonder: A Spiritual Anthology*, Samuel H. Dresner, ed. (New York: Crossroad, 2002), 81.

p. 88. *". . . Rabbi Zusya of Anipolye . . ."* Joseph Telushkin, *Jewish Literacy: The Most Important Things to Know about the Jewish Religion, Its People and Its History* (New York: William Morrow and Co., 1991), 242.

p. 90. *"O LORD, you have searched me and you know me. . . ."* Psalm 139:1,4.

p. 92. *"But he who looks into the perfect law . . . blessed in his doing."* James 1:25. RSV.

p. 93. *"[Moses] made the laver of copper and its stand of copper from the mirrors of the women. . . ."* Exodus 38:8, NJPS

p. 94. *"Now, amongst the Israelites were certain women, . . . to hear the details of the worship."* Discussion of contrasting Midrashic readings of Exodus 38:8 by both Ibn Ezra and Rashi can be found in Rav Alex Israel, "Vayakhel-Pikudei: Vanity Mirrors" in *Thinking Torah* at http://www.lind.org.il/features/vayakhel63.htm. See also Avivah Gottlieb Zornberg, *The Particulars of Rapture* (New York: Image/Doubleday, 2001), chapter one.

p. 95. *"Now we see but a poor reflection . . . even as I am fully known."* 1 Corinthians 13:12.

p. 97. ". . . *composing a song of deeds which only God understands.*"
Heschel, *I Asked for Wonder*, 59.

9
TRUTH: *Freedom in the Rough*

p. 100. "*Abraham's father was an idol-maker.* . . ."
This Midrash from Genesis Rabbah 38:13 is taken from *On The Nature of Being Human: An Ethics Sourcebook*, published by The Curriculum Institute, 164. Used with permission.

p. 104. "*Was it because / at last / I cleaned the window.* . . ." This poem was previously published in *Poetry*, May 2003, 70.

p. 105. "*You will know the truth, and the truth will make you free.*"
John 8:32. NASB.

p. 107. "*Take your son, your only son, Isaac* . . . *that will come through Isaac and become a great nation.*" Genesis 22:1–19.

pp. 109-110. "*The night we married, making love.* . . ." This poem was previously published in its full version as "Sestina Genesis" in a 2002 issue of *re:generation quarterly*.

10
CREATION: *A Fire in the Belly*

p. 115. "*Rabbi Simon said* . . . *'Man is already made.'*" This Midrash from Genesis Rabbah, VIII, 5 along with the interpretation I use here, can be found in Barry W. Holtz, "Midrash" in *Back To the Sources: Reading the Classic Jewish Texts* (New York: Touchstone, 1984), 191-192. Used with permission.

pp. 116-117. *"A man who had falsely slandered the rabbi in his town . . . has worked on me and my town."* This Midrash from the Talmud, Ketubot 103b, is found in *On the Nature of Being Human: An Ethics Sourcebook*, published by The Curriculum Institute, www.thecurriculum.org. Used by permission.

pp. 118-119. *"Into the rushing dark . . ."* This poem was previously published in a slightly different version as "Annunciation" in *Southern Poetry Review*, 42:2, Winter 2004, 38.

pp. 121-122. *"My soul doth magnify the Lord. . . ."* Luke 1:46–50. KJV.

11
REVELATION: *Word Without End*

pp. 126-127. *"While they were talking and discussing, Jesus himself came near. . . ."* Luke 24:15–21, 25–32. NRSV.

Glossary

Bet Midrash: Jewish study house.

Chutzpah: Unmitigated gall, brazenness beyond imagination.

Darshan: A writer or preacher of midrash, in ancient times always a rabbi.

Derash: A non-literal, imaginative interpretation of scripture.

Genizah: A burial place for worn or otherwise unusable Hebrew Bibles.

Haggadah: A service of Midrash texts read and enacted by Jewish families to accompany the Passover seder meal.

Hasidic Sermon: A set form of preaching in which two seemingly unrelated Bible verses are connected by the preacher's wit and wisdom to make a larger point. A form of midrash.

Hevruta: Friend, friendship, companionship, or connection; commonly used to mean a Torah study partner.

Kabbalah: An aspect of Jewish mysticism. It consists of a large body of speculation on the nature of divinity, the creation, the origin and fate of the soul, and the role of human beings.

Metaphor: A figure of speech in which a word or phrase that ordinarily designates one thing is used to designate another, thus making an implicit comparison.

Midrash: An ancient approach to scripture interpretation that employs imaginative tools such as story, metaphor, argument, and wordplay to search out hidden meaning in Bible texts.

Parable: A seemingly simple story suggesting a moral or religious lesson with multiple layers of meaning.

Parashiyot: A Hebrew term meaning "portions," which refers to the division of the Torah into fifty-two sections that in a Jewish synagogue are read and studied weekly in succession throughout the year.

Peshat: A literal, historically accurate, logic-minded interpretation of scripture.

Rabbi/Sage: Master or teacher; a Jewish title of respect or honor for a teacher of religious law.

Sha'ashu'a: Delight, pleasure, entertainment, play. Literally: the word for attention, doubled.

Shekinah: God's majestic presence or manifestation, which has descended to dwell among humans.

Svara: The human ethical impulse, comprised of equal parts gut instinct and informed learning.

Syntax: The pattern or formation of sentences or phrases in a language.

Talmud: The collection of ancient Rabbinic writings consisting of the Mishnah and the Gemara, constituting the basis of religious authority in Orthodox Judaism.

Teshuvah: A Hebrew word meaning at once return, response, and repentance.

Torah: The first five books of the Hebrew Scriptures, including the entire body of religious law and learning incorporating both sacred literature and oral tradition. Also called Oral Torah and Written Torah.

Yeshivah: A school for learning Torah and Talmud.

About Paraclete Press

Who We Are

Paraclete Press is an ecumenical publisher of books and recordings on Christian spirituality. Our publishing represents a full expression of Christian belief and practice—from Catholic to Evanglical, from Protestant to Orthodox.

Paraclete Press is the publishing arm of the Community of Jesus, an ecumenical monastic community in the Benedictine tradition. As such, we are uniquely positioned in the marketplace without connection to a large corporation and with informal relationships to many branches and denominations of faith.

We like it best when people buy our books from booksellers, our partners in successfully reaching as wide an audience as possible.

What We Are Doing

Books

Paraclete Press publishes books that show the richness and depth of what it means to be Christian. Although Benedictine spirituality is at the heart of all that we do, we publish books that reflect the Christian experience across many cultures, time periods, and houses of worship.

We publish books that nourish the vibrant life of the church and its people—books about spiritual practice, formation, history, ideas, and customs.

We have several different series of books within Paraclete Press, including the bestselling *Living Library* series of modernized classic texts; *A Voice from the Monastery*—giving voice to men and women monastics about what it means to live a spiritual life today; award winning literary faith fiction; and books that explore Judaism and Islam and discover how these faiths inform Christian thought and practice.

Recordings

From Gregorian chant to contemporary American choral works, our music recordings celebrate the richness of sacred choral music through the centuries. Paraclete is proud to distribute the recordings of the internationally acclaimed choir Gloriæ Dei Cantores, who have been praised for their "rapt and fathomless spiritual intensity" by *American Record Guide*, and the Gloriæ Dei Cantores Schola, which specializes in the study and performance of Gregorian chant. Paraclete is also the exclusive North American distributor of the Monastic Choir of St. Peter's Abbey in Solesmes, France, long considered to be a leading authority on Gregorian chant performance.

Learn more about us at our Web site:
www.paracletepress.com, or call us toll-free at
1-800-451-5006.

Other Titles on Judaism from Paraclete Press

Let Us Break Bread Together
A Passover Haggadah for Christians
Pastor Michael Smith and
Rabbi Rami Shapiro

$8.95, Trade Paper, 64 pages
1-55725-444-3

In this special book, co-authored by a rabbi and
a pastor, we have the unique opportunity to
experience an authentic Jewish Passover seder,
from a distinctively Christian perspective. This
haggadah offers meaningful insights on how
Christians can both learn from Judaism as a
means of deepening their Christian faith, and
better understand the Jewishness of Jesus.

How Firm a Foundation
A Gift of Jewish Wisdom for Christians and Jews
Rabbi Yechiel Eckstein

$16.95, Trade Paper, 270 pages
1-55725-189-4

This rich presentation of Jewish life, beliefs and
practices, festivals and holy days, rites of passage,
worship practice, and dietary laws is ideal for
Christians seeking a better understanding of
Judaism.

Mudhouse Sabbath
Lauren F. Winner

$17.95, Hardcover, 161 pages
1-55725-344-7

Lauren Winner illuminates eleven spiritual
practices from Judaism that shape her life as a
Christian. Whether discussing her own prayer
life, the spirituality of candle-lighting, or the
differences between the Jewish Sabbath or a
Sunday spent at the *Mudhouse*, her favorite coffee
shop, Winner writes with appealing honesty and
rare insight.

Available from most bookstores or through Paraclete Press:
www.paracletepress.com; 1-800-451-5006
Try your local bookstore first.